FAMILY
VALUES

FAMILY
VALUES

RESET TRUST, BOUNDARIES, AND CONNECTION WITH YOUR CHILD

DR. CHARLES SOPHY
WITH REBECCA RAPHAEL

SIMON ELEMENT

New York   London   Toronto   Sydney   New Delhi

SIMON ELEMENT

An Imprint of Simon & Schuster, Inc.
1230 Avenue of the Americas
New York, NY 10020

First Simon Element hardcover edition October 2022

SIMON ELEMENT is a trademark of Simon & Schuster, Inc.

For information about special discounts for bulk purchases, please contact Simon & Schuster Special Sales at 1-866-506-1949 or business@simonandschuster.com.

The Simon & Schuster Speakers Bureau can bring authors to your live event. For more information or to book an event, contact the Simon & Schuster Speakers Bureau at 1-866-248-3049 or visit our website at www.simonspeakers.com.

Interior design by Renato Stanisic

Manufactured in the United States of America

10 9 8 7 6 5 4 3 2 1

Library of Congress Control Number: 2022941309

ISBN 978-1-6680-0011-3
ISBN 978-1-6680-0013-7 (ebook)

CONTENTS

Foreword VII

Introduction XI

Part I: Finding the Reset Button

Chapter 1: Parenting with a New Lens 3

Chapter 2: Change Yourself, Change Your Child 19

Chapter 3: Understanding Your Baggage 35

Chapter 4: Toxic Power Dynamics 49

Chapter 5: Taking Stock of Your Parenting Style 71

Part II: Family Values in Action

Chapter 6: SWEEP 91

Chapter 7: The Five Essentials of Your Family Portrait 111

Chapter 8: Communicating and Connecting 131

CONTENTS

Chapter 9: The Most Important Role Model
Your Kids Will Ever Have   145

Chapter 10: Raising Confident, Capable Kids   155

Part III: New Starts and New Tests

Chapter 11: Negotiation and Motivation   169

Chapter 12: Evolving Families   185

Chapter 13: Lightning Round of Common Questions   203

Conclusion   225

Acknowledgments   233

Index   235

FOREWORD

Dr. Charles Sophy wrote *Family Values* because he truly *values family*. He recognizes that your family is the most precious, defining aspect of your entire life and is the yardstick by which you will—and should—measure your success in this world.

We all want our children to thrive and succeed in every possible way. *Family Values* is going to help ensure that comes to pass for you as a parent. Why? Because you and your family deserve it. All those good things that transpire in healthy, happy, functional families are not just for "other people." They're not just what you hear about or see on television or in a movie. Those beautiful things are for *you* and *your family*, and Dr. Sophy is here to help you recognize that, know it to the core of your being, and step up and claim what is rightfully yours.

Dr. Sophy—"Charlie" to all of us who have the privilege of working in the trenches alongside him—has always recognized that parents are raising adults, not children, and that *everything your child will ever be, they are now becoming*. He wants to help you do it right; he knows how to build on your God-given parental instincts, and, most important, he cares enough to tell you what you *need* to hear instead of what you *want* to hear.

Dr. Sophy speaks and writes plain truth, yet I've never heard him play the "blame game." You won't read a word of him pointing fingers at you in this book. I suspect you're doing some great things as a parent; he will help you embrace those parenting practices you need to keep. He'll also inspire you to change any that, based on results, aren't working. Most important, he truly gets it. He gets that parenting is *not even almost easy*, and this is *not* the world you grew up in. This post-pandemic, social media dominated, fast-paced world is a high-risk environment in which to raise children. I know that sounds terrible, but it just is. It's tough out there. It matters not whether you struggle to make ends meet or live in a mansion; the challenges spare no family. Dr. Sophy has seen and solved the problems facing parents all across the entire spectrum. He's a realist and knows you're not the only voice in your child's ear, so he's committed to making sure you are the *best* voice they hear. He will meet you where you are. No judgment, no lectures, no condemnation—just partnership.

Family Values isn't just a book, it's a manual. You'll probably wear out your first copy and go pick up another one. It's full of hands-on tools, and you're going to be really surprised at a few things you find. You'll read about how your children need acceptance, permanence, and freedom to be kids. Further, the good doctor is going to tell you precisely *how* to bring those critical factors to bear. Perhaps the biggest surprise is going to be how he's also dedicated to rejuvenating *you*, Mom and Dad. All this knowledge, skill, and work lifts so much weight off your shoulders so you can lead your family with joy, love, and confidence, because that's what you'll feel inside.

I'm excited for you and the journey you're about to take with my dear friend and colleague Dr. Charles Sophy and *Family Values: Reset Trust, Boundaries, and Connection with Your Child.*

Dr. Phil McGraw

FAMILY
VALUES

INTRODUCTION

Congratulations. You have just cracked open the last book you will ever need to have the secure, loving, joyful, lasting family you've always wanted. You're about to gain the tools that will get your family—starting with you—where you want and need to be. Now, your getting this tool kit and setting it into action may very well put me out of business, but if it gets your family to a stable, trusting, thriving place—which it will—nothing would gratify me more.

My name is Dr. Charles Sophy, and I am the former medical director of the Los Angeles County Department of Children and Family Services (DCFS), the largest child welfare system in the country. When a child's safety or well-being is in question, when the police have to get involved, or when it's obvious that a child is in danger, I'm called to step in. I'm the guy they turn to when the wheels have really fallen off the bus.

I'm also a physician in private practice who treats adults, children, and all kinds of families. I'm board-certified in three specialties: family practice, adult psychiatry, and child and adolescent psychiatry. Since I work with people of all ages, on the medical side as well as the mental health side, I take a holistic approach to assessing a situation and developing a plan that will get kids back on track.

It's my job to pinpoint the problems families face, forecast what may look innocent today but could blow up tomorrow, and provide a road map that will lead each family member and the unit as a whole to safety, health, and well-being.

When I meet a family, I look into everything. Whether I see a child who's acting out, a teen struggling with anxiety, parents at their wits' end, or an entire family in need of a serious course correction, I explore and treat all facets of their life. From ordering an MRI to performing psychological tests, running blood work, or putting hair follicles under a microscope, I look at all the factors that merge together—emotional, psychological, physical, or otherwise. I take nothing at face value, and only feel comfortable making a diagnosis and recommendations after understanding the patient as a whole human being. When a child comes to the attention of the Los Angeles County DCFS, I interface with that child in collaboration with the family, the child welfare system, and multiple other public and/or private agencies. More often than not, I'll need to make recommendations for that child as well as for other children and adults in the family. Treating the whole family will enable each individual member to feel the stability they need to thrive, which will, in turn, ensure the strength of the family. The bottom line: Any family unit is a system that's only as strong as its weakest member, and when there's work to be done, nobody gets a free pass.

There aren't always visible issues or scars on the outside that warrant my involvement, and far too often even the most well-meaning parents neglect to provide one of the most basic things that every child needs: a sense of stability. Every child deserves and craves that permanence, whether it stems from something as basic as a home free of neglect or from having a predictable structure, age-appropriate rules, and clear expectations. These are the fundamentals to making a child—and, frankly, an entire family—feel safe.

The problem is that many of us were not provided these essentials in our own formative years, and faced other challenges in our upbringing that have had long-lasting implications. Therefore, we simply do not have the tools or the role-modeling skills to offer them appropriately and fully to our children. As a result, we may not be able to understand, deal with, or even accurately identify conditions that could negatively affect our children. That's where I come in. The good news is, no matter what challenges you faced in your upbringing, you still can do better for *your* children. There is hope for your family no matter your background or current circumstances. I can practically hear you asking, "Are you sure? What if it's too late and I've already done this parenting thing all wrong?" It's not too late; it never is. And whatever mistakes you've made along the way, as we all have, we're going to acknowledge them, learn from them, and then have the know-how to do better. I've treated some of the most extreme, dramatic, and complicated family situations that exist. I also see a significant number of families who are doing the very best they can, day in and day out, yet have hit some kind of bump in the road. In every case, we start with the basics. There's always a safe and healthy way to move forward, no matter how complicated life has become or how out of whack your family dynamic feels. I've helped families in total disaster facing obstacles that seem insurmountable, and now I will help you every step of the way.

I'm in the trenches with you, and we'll get through this together. As I write this book, I have a sixteen-year-old son. I know all too well how hard and complicated parenting can be. I've been there, I'm there now, and I get it. Being in the roles of both doctor and parent is eye-opening; blended with my experience in the child welfare system, it's a rare perspective that I'm able to offer to you. I'll give you expert advice that's truly one-of-a-kind, because nobody else has sat in this seat before, serving all these roles simultaneously and for such a large population—upward of forty thousand children and families. So you can feel confident that you're in good hands.

I'm writing this in the middle of the Covid-19 pandemic, which has upended our lives in countless ways. This book was always intended to give you encouragement and the tools to hit the reset button so you can take a new approach with your parenting, but once the pandemic hit, every single family got slammed with an intense, challenging, life-changing new set of circumstances that none of us ever imagined. Living through a pandemic, no matter what ages your kids are, has substantially shaped countless aspects of their lives as well. You've had a front-row seat as it has unfolded, and now I'm here to guide you and your children as you move forward from the trauma. And make no mistake about it—even if life has resumed and feels normal again, for our kids this was traumatic.

The pandemic led to social isolation, loss, and complexities that none of us were prepared to deal with. We now have the data to show that online schooling was a failure in so many ways, household violence doubled, and the global incidence of anxiety and depression increased by 25 percent. For most families, the pandemic exacerbated problems they were already contending with, and also added a layer of hardship that hadn't previously existed. So it's more important to me than ever to share what I know about how you and your family can find a way back to each other—not simply returning to the family or the people you were before the pandemic but creating an even stronger, more secure foundation that will allow everyone to thrive.

To be sure, we as a society were experiencing worrisome trends long before the pandemic. Between the years 2007 and 2019, the United States saw a 13 to 15 percent rise in reports of adolescent depression and/or anxiety. Emergency room visits for various mental health reasons—including self-harm—increased during that time frame as well. Suicide rates leapt a staggering 60 percent from 2007 to 2018. We must pay attention to what America's adolescents and teens are silently screaming through their behavior, screams that grew louder during the Covid-19 pandemic. The isolation that all of us, but especially our adolescents and teens, endured through the pandemic has created wounds that must be healed in order to avoid lifelong scars.

It's vitally important that we as parents, educators, and medical and mental health professionals pay close attention to each and every adolescent and teen we encounter, both inside our home and out. Any change within their daily function—and, most important, any sign of withdrawal or isolation from normal life—must be seen as a red flag to be addressed immediately. This book is designed to provide simple but highly effective tools for assessing and tracking where parents, their children, and their families fall on the scale of daily function. These assessments will help determine whether behaviors fall into age-appropriate categories and will alert parents when it's time to take action. The tools will also highlight any areas that need to be strengthened and provide simple and effective ways to bolster those areas.

I'm not saying the work will be easy, but it's absolutely doable. The most critical ingredient is commitment from you. You must be committed, even though you're being pulled in every direction all the time. You already have another significant factor necessary for success: love for and devotion to your children. But it takes more than just good intentions, because you're not the only thing that's affecting your children. Given the current state of the world, you need to work toward being the *main* source of influence over your children's lives.

We're inundated with information, surrounded by an endless stream of content, and really don't have reliable ways to filter the messaging our kids are exposed to, no matter how hard we try. Many parents feel powerless to combat the influences that outside forces have on their children. They become paralyzed and just accept the damage. I say no. Absolutely not! You *can* counterprogram your children. You *can* give them new metrics for measuring their self-esteem aside from their number of followers. You don't need to allow your children to barely make eye contact with you because they're constantly glued to a screen. You don't have to accept as an inevitable sign of the times that your children get caught vaping in the school bathroom, tell you weed is just a plant, or come through your front door drunk in the middle of the night. You can—and you must—counteract these influences. You have the ability to reset the patterns and expectations that your kids follow instead of contributing to the craziness of our interconnected and fast-paced world, which has our kids paying the highest price of all. None of us should blindly accept perceived social norms as standards for our own family. Not in the midst of a pandemic, not in the aftermath of it, not ever.

Regardless of the situation, no matter what point you're at in your parenting journey or how far off base you think you may be, the knowledge and tools your family needs—which I'm about to give you—will steer you toward success. Of course, every family is different and defines that success in their own way, so there's no one-size-fits-all approach. But after working with tens of thousands of adults and kids of all ages, including in my practice, within the welfare system, and on the *Dr. Phil* show, I have seen and understand the most common pitfalls as well as the values that every family needs to be strong. You don't have to get to a place of crisis like many of the families I see, and you won't if you listen up.

This book is called *Family Values* because it will help your family get back onto the same page when it comes to the central questions that define us, sustain us, strengthen us, and enrich us:

- Who are we as a family?
- What is most important to us?
- What connects us to each other?
- Why do we want to be a family?
- What will make the work we have to do together worth it?
- What value will it have in the long term?

Together, we'll work to clearly articulate and implement what your family values, the principles you hold most sacred, and in the process of doing that, we'll be adding infinitely to your family values, their worth, now and for decades to come.

If you were to ask me, "Dr. Sophy, how do I create a fabulous, close, happy, and healthy family?" the first thing I'd ask in response is, "Where are you now?" That's our starting point. A solid family isn't one that's grounded in denial and fooling ourselves. We need to assess the current situation—what's working, what's not, and everything in between. Only then can we figure out how we can fix it, and then explore what to get rid of, embrace, or maintain to help your family rehabilitate and succeed for the long haul. How do you want to parent differently than your own parents did? Why? How has your parenting style been affected by those goals? What changes would you like to make going forward? Things in your household may have started out similarly to those in every other pretty good family in America, but along the way you likely hit some stumbling blocks that might have set you on a different track. Or you may have picked up this book because your family is in crisis, and you know that's my specialty. No matter what you've been through or where you find yourself now, the power to hit the reset button is yours. At any time, you can change the way you're raising your children. With deliberate thought and action, you can redirect your family to thrive.

There are good reasons why any one of us finds ourselves struggling—none of which should make us feel guilty, overwhelmed, or judged. None of us gets a handbook on how to be a parent or how to guide a family toward success and safety. That's about to change. The outcome you want—a reset button that allows you to realign your real-life parenting moments with the values you hold dear—doesn't happen without your full understanding and full participation. But I can guarantee that it will happen when you have a plan in place to fall back on when life throws you curveballs. I have seen it happen with thousands of families, and I believe deeply that it will happen with yours when you commit to the process. Consider this book your planning process for getting your family values back to the center of how your family operates—both as a group and for each individual.

Whether I was working with the most at-risk population through the Los Angeles County DCFS or helping more seemingly picture-perfect families in my private practice, the themes were quite similar. Children have basic needs that must be met for them to develop healthy self-esteem and the confidence they need to move through the world, and it's a parent's job to meet them. No matter what parenting style you have, regardless of your children's ages, despite your round-the-clock schedule at work as you try to make ends meet, or any other factors at play in your life, I know that your children need these from you:

Acceptance. Your kids need to know you love them for who they are as a precursor to their own self-acceptance and confidence. When they know they're accepted by the most important person and role model in their life, they not only learn to love themselves but also have a healthy starting point for building positive relationships.

Structure. Children need the predictability and calmness of a schedule for eating, sleeping, playing, and more. When their life is organized and they feel a sense of control, their fears and anxieties are reduced. This isn't about living according to a strict schedule, and I certainly don't mean that the entire foundation of your family will crumble if you miss a family dinner here or there. I'm talking about basic consistency so that when your children venture into the world, they come from a place of safety and confidence, not concern that each day is a new puzzle to be solved with no pieces in place from the previous day, and the day before that, as a head start.

Freedom to Be a Kid. When children are "parentified" at an early age, meaning they're put in the role of having to act like a parent, they're denied the essential experiences of youth. Kids need to be kids. (And parents need to parent, which is a whole chapter in the pages ahead.) That's not to say that you should deprive them of independence or that they don't need responsibilities as they grow up; not at all. One of your goals is to encourage that, in fact. But kids need the freedom to spend their childhood finding their own unique paths to success and happiness. When kids have burdens unduly placed upon them, like being a family caregiver or provider, they often regress later in life.

These concepts are foundational to building your child's health and self-esteem, to setting them up to be productive and confident as they get the most out of their lives. As basic as these pillars seem, they can be complicated to uphold, especially when life throws up unexpected roadblocks. So in this book I will load up your tool kit so you can tackle what's in front of you now, see around corners before problems escalate, and give your family a new foundation that will remain solid for years to come. I'll talk you through the hazards that I've seen too many families stumble through, and together we'll practice noticing the warning signs so you can avoid them. Because the work we do here is not just to put out fires—part of it is about recognizing or avoiding danger signs, and learning how to proactively create and follow a road map that takes you to the best place for you and your family is equally important. We'll certainly do those things, too.

Together we'll create a step-by-step plan of action for leading your family so you know you're trending toward success every day. The work I'll teach you how to do will require you to be open to exploring the responsibility you might have to take for some of the problems, and the leadership role you'll likely need to assume for all the change. You're in this parenting relationship for the long haul, so if you truly want the generations coming after you to live in happier and healthier ways, know that the work we'll do together throughout this book is going to change that trajectory for the better.

To be absolutely clear, nowhere in this book will I ask you to point fingers, take blame, or feel failure. Parenting is hard. Each and every family has faced unbelievable obstacles that have made it incredibly difficult to keep everybody on track. You as an individual parent and you as a team member to another coparent need to adopt and be comfortable with a guilt-free parenting stance, where the work that you do to understand how you got to this point is done from a place of acceptance and safety—the same essentials that your child needs from you to get back on track. That means that you won't be litigating how the problems you're looking to resolve got started, pointing fingers of blame, or suffering a penalty. You'll be examining the roots of your parenting style in order to understand where change needs to begin. That means accepting that you and your parenting partner, if you have one, came together to build this family and to make it the best it can be. That is the reason you're re-structuring and resetting the family dynamic now. Life is a learning process, and we all have our own histories and baggage. As part of that journey, now is the time for you and your parenting partner to shift the values of your family to a greater place.

So there's no need to feel bad about what may seem like harsh-ness in this new style of parenting, or the guilt of saying no and meaning no. Parenting from your family values means that there are clear boundaries around behaviors that are not acceptable, even if they've been permitted in the past. The more your children react in a negative way to your new method of doing business, the more you need to see that as the proof you needed to undertake this process. As the families mentioned throughout this book will show you, you may be saving your kids' lives and the lives of the future generations in your family.

Whether you know it or not, your children are becoming everything they will ever be right now. Everything you're doing or not doing at this moment will affect your family's legacy. So let's not waste any time. You've already put yourself on a path to success by picking up this book and partnering with me. You chose this book because you care about your children and you want action-oriented advice. Don't die for your children; live for them. Your role as a parent is the highest calling you'll have in your life. No matter what brought you to this moment, you will rise to the challenge once you have the know-how. It's time for your family to be the best it can be right now and for future generations. Get ready to see your family thrive as you live in accordance with your values. It's all up to you, no matter where you are right now. It's never too late to hit the reset button. Let's get started.

PART I

Finding the Reset Button

CHAPTER 1

Parenting with a New Lens

Nicholas was a tenth-grade student who was having trouble sleeping. His mother, who thought her sixteen-year-old was suffering from depression, took him to doctors who prescribed sleep aids and antidepressants, which Nicholas refused to take. However, he had tried using marijuana with a friend, and told his mom it made him feel better. Desperate to help her son feel good and afraid to alienate him further, Nicholas's mother decided to get a medical marijuana card for herself, buy the drug weekly, and illegally give it to her son, whose teenage brain was still very much in development.

After slacking at his previous school, Nicholas had been put in an alternative high school, where he wasn't doing well academically, didn't participate in any extracurricular activities, and had only a few friends, all of whom smoked weed. Then he stopped going to class altogether. He stopped giving his parents updates on where he was at night. The situation was getting worse. Finally, the tipping point:

Dispatcher: Hello, you've reached the Los Angeles County Department of Children and Family Services Child Protection Hotline.
Caller: Hi, my name is [Mr. James], and I'm the principal of [Alternative High School]. I'm calling with concerns about

one of our students. He's been absent more than he's been here, his grades have fallen, he looks disheveled when he comes to school, and I'm worried he's using drugs and/or alcohol. We've reached out to his parents several times and they assure me that they will take care of it, but they clearly haven't. We've tried to speak with him at school, but he's become increasingly belligerent and unresponsive to us. And when we do approach him to talk about what's going on, he won't show up to school for days afterward. It's obvious something is wrong, and we're all very worried about him.

Dispatcher: A few questions, sir. Do you know if he's had any mental health history, has he ever been arrested, what is his current living situation, and are there other children in the home?

Caller: Within school hours, there have been no additional signs of mental health concerns. I believe he lives at home with his parents and his younger brother.

Dispatcher: Do you have that address, sir?

That was the call that triggered a visit by DCFS to Nicholas's home, as is protocol for a situation such as this. It's quite common for school administrators to reach out to experts like me for help. In Nicholas's case, that transcript and recording were all the information I had before a pretty stylish, albeit slightly unkempt, teenager with spotty facial hair entered my office a few days later. The instant he walked in with his parents, I could sense a well-established power dynamic that was off-kilter. His mom wasn't seen or respected as a parent. She seemed to fear her son or to be seeking his approval, perhaps to compensate for what was missing in her marriage. His dad seemed meek, out of sorts, and almost intimidated by both his wife and his son.

I told Nicholas that before I could help him, he would need to get sober. Nicholas was not game, to say the least, and we struggled because nothing made him feel as good as the marijuana to which he'd become accustomed. Since he wasn't willing to quit on his own, I had him start on a more aggressive, structured path. He reluctantly attended an outpatient facility where he worked with a sobriety coach. It was a battle every day. He snuck in weed and skipped sessions, and when he did attend, he was often mentally shut down or too angry to productively participate. Finally, after lots of drama, more police involvement, psychiatric emergency teams (PET), parental pleading, crying, and tons of anger on all sides, we got Nicholas admitted to an inpatient substance abuse rehabilitation center. After he completed and came out of his first inpatient stint, his life had more stability. He still wasn't hitting on all cylinders— he wasn't always getting up in the morning and continued to skip class—but at least he was sober and going to therapy. Unfortunately, it didn't take long before he surrendered to his old coping skill of self-medicating by smoking pot multiple times daily. Part of the issue was that the feelings he was trying to fight off all came back when he returned home. Another factor was that his favorite way to self-medicate was constantly right before his eyes, thanks to both his friends and his mom. In his mind, he had an easy fix that gave him some relief and made him feel better in the moment, and that's all that mattered. But the damage he was doing to himself—and to his family unit—had to be stopped.

Throughout this time, I made several home visits, which is how I discovered that there was, unsurprisingly, more going on at home than just Nicholas's struggle. After holding a powerful position at a taxing job, Nicholas's father hadn't worked for years. Not only was he going through a depression but he also began inexplicably falling down in the house. Doctors had found no real reasons for his falling; he hadn't had a stroke, and there were no physical ailments that would cause his stumbles. It was a mystery.

Nicholas's mother became aggressively resentful and began acting out her frustrations and fears. The night Nicholas came home from his third time in rehab, his mother impulsively decided she wanted to get a tattoo. A cup filled with tequila in hand, she got a ride straight from work to the tattoo parlor. When she got to the parlor she was out of it, but still got the tattoo and managed to get another ride to their home—or close to it. A few hours later, no one knew where she was. Nicholas's father panicked and woke up Nicholas and his ten-year-old brother, asking if they thought their mother was all right, because she hadn't made it home. No one in the house got any sleep that night. At 4:30 a.m., a twentysomething with a skateboard knocked on the door. He was holding up Nicholas's mother, whom he'd found five houses down the street covered in mud and grass, still wearing her work outfit. She had gotten so drunk that she'd stumbled out of her taxi at the wrong house and passed out on a neighbor's lawn.

In the course of my work with this family, I gained insight into the full picture of what Nicholas and his family were truly experiencing. After losing his job, Nicholas's dad didn't know what his place was inside or outside the home. His own mother had been the primary disciplinarian in his household, while his father was the sole breadwinner who didn't interact much at home. With those as his only frames of reference about his identity and role, he was lost. We eventually came to find out that Nicholas's father was falling down to get attention from his family. That's how desperate, depressed, and off-course he was. When he lost his job, he lost himself.

We also came to learn that Nicholas's mother had substance abuse and mental health issues in her genetics; her brother was an addict. Siblings of addicts are often invisible victims, and this was the case for Nicholas's mother growing up. She suffered in silence while her parents' efforts—financial, emotional, and intellectual—were directed primarily if not exclusively toward her brother. Whether Nicholas's mom's mindset was "I sure won't parent like what I saw as a kid!" or a self-assured "That'll never happen to my family," it was no guarantee of preventing a similar outcome under her roof. Now that her own son was the one struggling, Nicholas's mother was in denial about it. It's important to be honest and up front with kids when the disease of addiction runs in the family; they need to know if they have a genetic propensity toward substance abuse that will be difficult for them to control or might harm them. But Nicholas's mother was falling into the same patterns of secrecy and acting out that she had seen modeled in her own family growing up, rather than establishing the boundaries, stability, and role-modeling her son needed.

Even though there was never any violence or abuse, and Nicholas was not neglected, he wasn't being parented. His parents' families had a history of underparenting, and because of that Nicholas's parents didn't have a clear idea of how to break those patterns. As a result, neither Nicholas nor his brother were raised with a sense of stability. In fact, as the firstborn, *he* was the one who had to act like a parental figure to his younger sibling. It was no wonder that Nicholas's behavior caught the eye of his high school principal and raised red flags; he didn't have clear boundaries or healthy role models showing him nondestructive coping mechanisms. The hurts, fears, and discomforts that his own parents were still processing made it that much more difficult for Nicholas to recognize when he was in a tough spot and then commit to his own healing work.

Where the Work Begins

I share this story about Nicholas and his family because it's a powerful and dramatic example of what a child's basic needs are, what can happen when they aren't met, and how we need to shift the way we think about what we perceive as our children's issues. In my twenty-two years as medical director of DCFS, the two words we used most often to help thousands of families understand what was missing from their homes were "safety" and "permanence." Whether those foundations are disrupted by divorce, perfectionism, sexuality, illness, homelessness, drugs, or the countless other variables that can hit with or without warning makes no difference in the end result. Without safety and permanence, nothing else I write in this book matters because your family value diminishes exponentially—but never irreparably, so roll up your sleeves.

Physical safety is making sure your children feel confident that they are protected by you and not in danger from you. Children who spend time anticipating physical danger—violence, exposure to traumatic experiences, physical abuse—are unable to establish a secure sense of self.

Emotional safety refers to a state a child is given to live in where relationships have attachment and predictability. Emotional safety means that the adults as well as the children are free to be vulnerable and open with their emotions, and everyone feels comfortable showing their authentic selves.

Permanence is the promise we make to our children that they will always have a family unit. It means that we provide our children with a safe and stable environment that will remain even when they may not be able to perceive it.

In Nicholas's case, his physical and emotional safety were in question because his parents let him smoke marijuana and skip school, and basically put him in a position where he was calling his own shots. He had no predictable schedule or emotional grounding either. He watched his parents argue constantly, and he overpowered his mom, who wanted to be his friend rather than his parent. Kids may act like they want to shake off their parents' control, but that's not what they actually desire. It's too much power for them to usurp, so they feel unsafe. There might be moments when they feel victorious for grabbing the reins, but all in all it rocks them when the grown-ups who are supposed to be in charge can't be counted on to do their job. It doesn't just shatter their senses of safety and permanence in the present; there are also potential long-term consequences such as a "failure to launch," as when young adults find it difficult to transition into adulthood or regress to the point that their maturity doesn't develop.

I always tell parents to look out for this when they ask for my help: Just because you bring "troubled" little Jimmy in to see me doesn't always mean that little Jimmy is the source of the problem. Often, families come to me with the belief that if I could just "fix" Jimmy, the parents' world would be at peace. But I have some news for you: Little Jimmy may seem as if he's the lightning rod in your family, but most likely he isn't. Rather, he's probably the member of your family who acts out the feelings and unmet needs of all the members at his own expense.

In stories such as these, we call the Nicholases and Jimmys the Identified Patient (IP). The IP is usually the emotionally youngest family member, who becomes a receptacle for any and all family members' unwanted feelings. While the IP may not be the youngest member of the family according to chronological age, they are often the person who is most sensitive to or least able to cope with a sense of imbalance or lack of security.

In Nicholas's case, it was clear to me that he wasn't the only member of his family whose needs were unmet and who needed healing. His behavior at school caused him to be identified as the IP, but that was simply because the rest of the family's struggles weren't as immediately apparent, and his parents weren't subject to the same oversight that he was.

Uncomfortable feelings for any family member are funneled through and projected onto the IP in many forms, most commonly as gaslighting, blame, or pressure to play a role in the family that the IP is likely not prepared to play. However, no matter how these emotions are projected onto the IP and no matter what, specifically, those feelings are, the result is almost always the same: the IP will respond to a lack of familial safety by acting out. Their behavior then reinforces the belief that they're the one who has the problem, when in fact the Identified Patient is typically the crutch who carries the heavy load of the family. In taking on this identity, he or she unknowingly becomes the enabler who allows the rest of the family to let other issues go unexamined. So while the IP's behavior is often what leads the family to connect with someone like me, the pertinent work typically starts elsewhere.

To be clear: None of this is to imply that the IP doesn't also have work to do or that the IP lacks accountability for their own actions. Not at all. But it's important to understand that there are more pieces to the puzzle of long-term recovery and change. Believe it or not, I've seen in many cases how children will become the parent because they have evolved more and are more mature. These are the more complex cases when it comes to shifting behavior.

I'm suggesting that instead of asking yourself "How can I fix my kid?" you might think, "What could be exacerbating the problems we're seeing—and what's my role?" In Nicholas's case, his parents' own issues were trickling down to him, the IP, as they inevitably do in every home. Nicholas was making poor choices and had work to do, but he needed his family to take on their own work for everyone's situation to improve.

Healing from Within

When I met Nicholas's family, they had no idea how they—and more specifically, their parenting—were products of their learning history. By doing an audit of their generational legacy, including both their strengths and needs, they began to understand what they had brought into their chaotic home with two children.

For example, Nicholas's dad appreciated that his own father modeled for him the value of hard work; he was proud that he, too, had a solid work ethic. So it made all the sense in the world to him why being unemployed left him shattered. Nicholas's mom began to unpack what it was like growing up in a home colored by addiction, and how her fear of tackling it head-on left both her and Nicholas running right back into the same issues. With that self-awareness and more, we took a no-holds-barred look at how these two parents could begin to heal from their baggage. We were able to speak candidly about how to break the cycles from their upbringing that they were perpetuating as parents, and how to use their hard-earned knowledge to set an entirely new precedent for their kids. We got specific about what they wanted as a family, and then both parents began to ask themselves, "Is what I'm doing in the best interests of my kids and bringing me closer to that vision of success?"

We did, thankfully, get Nicholas the sustainable help he needed to stay sober, at which point everyone was in a better place to hear what he really needed most of all: to feel a sense of safety and permanence. He needed to have those most basic needs met so he could get the chance to stop being a parent and start being a teenager. The last time I saw Nicholas he was still a bit unkempt and needed a shave, but he was sober, aware of boundaries, and in school. It wasn't a straight line toward a fantasy of happily ever after; of course not. There are always bumps in the road and challenges to tackle. His parents didn't need to be perfect, nor did he. None of us does. But we do need tools in our arsenal, starting with this new vocabulary and framework for how we think about parenting.

The Solution Starts with You

When you become a parent, you create the foundation of a new family. But none of us ever starts with a clean or untarnished slate. We all bring what we have from our past, and all our understandings about how things are supposed to work or not supposed to work.

Family is the most influential piece shaping us all. The good things about you and the bad things about you, what you like about yourself and what you wish were different, what you pat yourself on the back for and what you beat yourself up over were all somehow shaped by your family and the way you grew up.

Going one step further, a child's brain is basically constructed through a process that begins early in life and continues into adulthood. When you're born, your brain is built on simpler circuits, and eventually more complex brain circuits will build on them. Family history and your genes provide the basic blueprint for your brain development, but experiences, especially essential early life experiences, influence how or whether genes are expressed. Together, they establish either a sturdy or a fragile base for your brain, and for all the learning, health, and behavior that will follow. The ability of your brain to reorganize and adapt is greatest in the first years of your life and decreases with age. So when a child experiences any type of trauma—whether it be abuse, watching parents fight too often, or the repercussions of a pandemic—it can stunt brain growth and development. On the flip side, when children feel safe and nurtured and have positive experiences that help them heal, negative neurological effects are minimized and healthy brain development is promoted.

As you grow up, your family life continues to reinforce the templates you'll use for life in too many aspects to count. For example, we develop preconceived notions of how people communicate with one another. If you were raised in a household where your parents were passive-aggressive toward each other and toward you, what you witnessed for decades will surface in terms of how you speak to your coworkers, your spouse, and your kids. Or perhaps your parents only lavished you with praise and attention if you consistently made the dean's list. Without top marks, your self-worth and their love were in question. That, too, leaves an impact. On the flip side, if you grew up hearing things such as "You're worthless," "You can't possibly win," or "College? Forget it, you'll never make it," I can guarantee that you now have wiring that makes it more likely for you to produce the same thing: a self-doubting child who grows into an adult without the foundation or sense of self that will allow them to guide their family.

Our concepts of trust, definition of self, and so much more are shaped by our upbringing. If you didn't feel safe showing your parents the real you, or if you felt compelled to keep your parents seemingly happy by presenting only the "best" parts of who you are, you undoubtedly have developed coping strategies (some useful, others not in the least), learned to compartmentalize (for better or worse), and internalized messaging about what is and isn't okay about you (a narrative you've hopefully begun to question).

We all have our baggage—every single one of us. Dropping it at the door when you leave home, fall in love, start a family, or at any other point along the way isn't an option. Many people think that if they move geographically or make some physical change, it can erase the scars, modify the facts, or extricate them from being part of their family. That's not how it works. What you have to do is open up the bags and take a good, hard look at what's in them. You must take an inventory of what you're dealing with and then identify what you want to keep, clean out, and add as you move forward, now that you're a parent and can do things differently. Yes, your family of origin is an incredibly powerful influence, but you aren't bound by it. Some of the most important work of our lifetime is to deliberately take the opportunity to pick the good, discard the not so good, and use whatever we want and need to build our own toolbox that will make our new family system better.

What does that actually mean, though? Exploring our past experiences of physical safety, emotional safety, and familial permanence is a lot more complicated than spring cleaning. Of course, we can't just clean out or discard anything we've been through with our families of origin because it's part of us, so I don't mean that literally. We can, however, process it, find meaning from it, develop strength and clarity from it, reframe it, and build upon it, making that foundation rock solid for our own kids. If you have a spouse or a parenting partner, this is a new lens for both of you to embrace. You'll each need to gain clarity about how your respective childhoods have influenced who you are and how you approach parenting, and then work together to create an amalgamation that responds to both of your upbringings and serves your joint parenting goals.

That fact is the reason why I keep saying that the key to every successful family system is you. Parenting begins with you—specifically, your emotional and physical health. Think about the oxygen masks on an airplane. What do they always tell you to do? Put the mask on yourself before assisting others. You need to take care of yourself and make sure you're safe before you can really help anyone else. It's the same in life. You can only help your family when you are healthy and stable. Is your foundation, like that of a house, as smooth and solid as it could be? Or are you still haunted by the cracks and the holes of your past experiences and traumas? Is a blemished base the template not only for your own self-esteem, self-worth, and self-beliefs but now also for those of your kids? No matter what's going on your home right now, it's not too late to build and rebuild, as long as that foundation gets stronger each time. It's time to let go of any guilt and get comfortable with the fact that what's happening is happening. Hear what I'm saying right now: grab onto a new and different system of beliefs. The work you do for yourself and your family will turn things around. It all starts with you.

CHAPTER 2

Change Yourself, Change Your Child

The tools I'm about to share will empower you to be a family leader who can look inward, set boundaries, build trust, and do what it takes to give your child the sense of safety and permanence they long for. For you to be successful in this endeavor, you must truly believe in the value of getting to the other side. Don't throw yourself into this work because you're angry. Don't do it because you're embarrassed by how far off course things have gotten, or how public an incident might have been. If you're motivated by fear of a very scary near miss, be grateful that you have a second chance now. Any decision to move forward in this process made out of anger is sure to fail, because once the anger subsides, the drive and motivation from that anger also dissipate. That's why it's important to make sure you're coming into the decision to do better from both your head and your heart. I will show you how to do the same kind of self-assessment that the other parents in this book took themselves and their families through. I'll show you how to perform the lens cleaning you need to accurately view your family dynamics and understand where they need to change. These steps are personal, and they'll help you come out of the process a more solid and comfortable parent.

I often hear from parents, "Dr. Sophy, there's nothing that you're going to tell me to do that I haven't already tried. My child doesn't listen, isn't afraid, and doesn't care what I say. They ignore all the boundaries, all the threats, and I eventually just give up. It's no use trying, and it's too late for a change."

I'll tell you the same thing I tell them: Yes, it's still worth trying, and no, it's never too late. However, the older your child, the longer it may take to make the necessary changes to their behavior. No matter their age, it won't happen unless you make an earnest commitment to doing what needs to be done. A halfhearted effort will continually give you a bigger problem than the one you started with. So you must focus and make a 100 percent commitment within yourself to understand what needs to be done and then take action.

The techniques suggested for you to transform outcomes have been generated from both scientifically and clinically proven trials and many years of adjustment based on experience. If you commit to them and follow them, you're almost guaranteed to get the behavioral outcomes you seek.

Parenting Begins with You

Let me give you an example of what it looks like to me when a parenting couple needs to align with themselves first to transform the troubling behavior of a child.

Carl and Erica had been married for fifteen years and came to me looking for help for their fourteen-year-old son, Scott. He was in eighth grade at the time, and until the school year that we met, Scott had done well academically and socially. He was a star swimmer at his previous school. He also played soccer on a championship team. But over the previous several months, Scott's schoolwork had declined and his friend group changed. When he was home, he isolated himself in his room, was more irritable and short-tempered, and refused to follow any rules or meet expectations. Also, his behavior with his younger siblings was dangerous and out of control. All of this was outside of the norm for Scott.

After meeting with both parents and Scott, together and separately, I saw clearly that Scott was a well-adjusted boy who truly enjoyed his life, but he'd recently become angry and shut down. He was pretty articulate about why the way his parents handled him upset him, as did their home life in general. It wasn't a big leap for anyone to understand that he was acting that anger out toward his family. It was also clear to me that Carl and Erica each needed to clear the lenses through which they were parenting and get on the same parenting page regarding what outcomes should be expected from their children. The next meeting that I set up with Carl and Erica alone was to begin the self-inventory process and hopefully define their wants and needs as individuals, as a couple, and as a couple that is a parenting team. I asked them to identify their joint parenting goals before coming into the meeting. As soon as we sat down, the conversation was taken over by Erica. I could tell that Carl was becoming increasingly angry and disengaged as his wife continued to speak at both him and me. From Erica's perspective, there was no place or room for dialogue; this was her monologue.

As I watched this dynamic unfold, I could see Carl becoming quite hot under the collar, turning red and sweating. His body language was also sending a message that he was uncomfortable. It didn't take long before Carl interrupted Erica's one-sided conversation to politely ask if he could add some comments. His wife quickly shut him down, saying she knew Scott better and therefore gave the better information and perspective.

Erica continued talking nonstop. Carl started to stutter and became exasperated and defeated. He then withdrew for the remainder of his wife's monologue. That was all I needed to know about why Scott was behaving the way he was. Anyone, much less a child who has to witness their parents treating each other in this manner, would reach a boiling point. As Scott had to endure his mother's spiraling and tolerate his parents' flawed relationship and communication, he must have felt like he was tied down to a chair next to a ticking bomb, helpless to do anything. He was acutely aware of his own voice being silenced, or of himself choosing to silence it, or both. How unbearably painful and difficult. His parents desperately needed to realign their own parenting goals before they could ever have a hope of implementing the consistent, predictable strategies required to transform Scott's behavior.

There's a reason why my catchphrase is "Parenting begins with you." Believe it or not, you have all the power to be the most influential change agent in your child's life. You may not feel so powerful when your child feels or acts out of control, but even in those darkest moments, you are. To make any significant shift in your child's behavior, change needs to first happen within you. And as I said, being a change agent for yourself, your child, and your family requires a 100 percent commitment. Remember, you didn't become you overnight. You've evolved through many years of life experiences in conjunction with predispositions from your DNA. And now that you know that any behavioral shift you're seeking in your child and family begins within you, there's a small mountain to climb known as the initial self-exploration phase, the essential first step in the process. We can't set our children up for success until we're clear about where we're coming from and what success truly means for ourselves.

You're probably not even aware that with every interaction you have with your child, you're setting an example for them and eliciting feelings in your child for them to understand and process. This affects their self-esteem and creates their feelings of self-worth. It's vitally important that you understand how you're impacting your child's formulation of their own sense of self. They need us to be able to create a safe space for their own growth—even if that's not a luxury we ourselves had. They take what they've integrated from their interactions with you and apply all they've learned when they venture into the world. Overall, it's your job to help your child navigate what's ahead; the stronger and healthier the interactions at home, the stronger and healthier the child you release into the world. And remember, that child you send out into the world is reflecting what you've role-modeled all those years.

Too often, parents have lost confidence in their own ability to assess what a situation calls for. It can be a challenge if you're feeling societal pressure to accept certain behaviors that don't sit right with you, or if your kid is telling you they need something that may not be common in your community. So the one statement I find myself saying quite often to parents is, "Don't overthink it." Your child and their behavior are not nearly as complicated as they seem or feel to you. If your gut is telling you that something is off, it probably is. If your instincts are telling you that your child needs something, even if it's not what you expected, you need to pay attention to those instincts. Think simply, act conservatively, and nine out of ten times you'll achieve the outcome you were seeking with your child. It's when a parent overthinks or overreacts that things become complicated and confusing for both parent and child.

You Are the Change Agent

Lisa, the mother of a six-year-old boy named Dash, called me one day asking if I could help her with him. Dash wouldn't follow her directions at home and often cursed at her when she pushed him to follow her orders. For example, there was always an argument when it was time to eat, shower, do homework, or get ready for bed. She had no recollection of why or when this started happening. All she knew was that she had regularly found herself in a battle over the prior several months. She had tried everything she knew how to do, from punishment to buying him whatever he wanted if he did what she asked, but still he rebelled.

When I met with Lisa and Dash the following day, they both were in the room together, and I think Dash may have said two or three sentences in the whole hour. It wasn't because he didn't want to talk; it was because he *couldn't* talk. Lisa overtook the room with her strong feelings about his behavior. There was almost no positive self-talk or discussion of any of Dash's positive attributes. There was also very little sense of how her role as the parent might be a factor in the situation.

I asked them to come back for another appointment five days later. At this next meeting, Lisa seemed even angrier than when we'd met previously. I asked her to sit and listen to Dash and me speak. I could tell she didn't like that request, but she complied. She wasn't comfortable with Dash having any sense of power or being given any level of respect by an adult. Her not liking the request told me that she must do a self-inventory to better understand what she was bringing to the relationship. Her parenting was being negatively influenced by her childhood and past experiences. Without self-awareness and the meaningful discoveries that can come from a self-inventory, she saw her son through a very cloudy lens. How unfair, unhealthy, and undesirable for all.

I began an age-appropriate conversation with Dash, telling him what kind of doctor I am and getting his take on why he thought we were meeting and how he felt about it. I also wanted to hear his thoughts on our previous meeting and understand what he saw as his role, including how he could make the situation at home better from his end. He was very clear and concise in all his responses. We talked about some of the rough spots that he participated in and how he wanted things fixed. It seemed the more appropriate he was and the more solution-oriented his responses, the more irritated Lisa got. When I asked him what he thought he and other family members could do to make things work better, he gave me specifics about what would help him follow instructions, including not being yelled at by his mom when she became frustrated. I could honestly understand how Dash felt in the past and how he was feeling that day, especially when I saw the way that his mom was responding to him. He also gave me some good ideas from his perspective about what he thought each of his family members could do, including his younger siblings, to help their family. I asked Dash if there was anything I hadn't asked him or that he felt I should know before I excused him so I could talk to Lisa alone. He said no, and at that point he walked out to wait in my waiting room.

As soon as the door closed, Lisa looked at me and said, "What the hell was that?"

I was shocked. I looked at her as if I had no idea what she was talking about and responded, "I'm not sure what you're referring to."

She said, "If I have to sit and listen to him tell me what he thinks is right or wrong, we can just forget about it now." It was the saddest response she could have given, but at the same time it was the most telling response. Lisa wasn't in a place where she was able to recognize or examine her role in changing the dynamic she had with her own son. Lisa's refusal to do a self-inventory and actively participate in the necessary internal work that then impacted Dash and the rest of the family meant that she likely would not be the change agent her family needed her to be.

My point in sharing that story is that if parents aren't ready to attempt to understand themselves and undo some of the entanglements that are consciously and unconsciously impacting their parenting style, they will likely end up in a family dynamic that's imbalanced and unhappy. And too often, what I see is that those dynamics are closely related to issues from their own childhoods and parenting models. My sincere hope is that Lisa will come around, and that the sessions we had will have planted the seeds of change, even if they take a little while to grow. But I also know how urgently important it is to do the work, uncomfortable though it may be; the longer it takes, the further apart families can get.

There's no way around it: You have to do the work on yourself so you don't get stuck in patterns you don't understand or are afraid to disrupt. Once that self-inventory work is completed, and you and your partner have fully committed to what you're learning in this book and to doing it to the best of your ability, you and your family are in for a very positive and pleasant shift in behavior and overall happiness.

Let's assume that most of us want to do that self-inventory and clear the lens through which we're looking at our children so we can get the desired outcome from their behavior. With that assumption, it's crucial to have both parents do this work within themselves and then get on the same page so there is only one agreed-upon outcome and one agreed-upon process by which to achieve it. Until you're both on the same page with your parenting objectives and goals, you run the risk of sending mixed messages that will only confuse children and leave a vacuum for the power dynamic to get disrupted. That's why it's so important to commit to using the tools in this book that will give you the clarity and focus to clearly establish and uphold the standards and values you hold most dear. I'm not trying to scare you—I'm just telling you the facts: The families who ended up in my care at DCFS didn't do their self-inventories, didn't clean their lenses, and didn't have a lucid road map for change. Period. That's when the system steps in to catch a child who needs a substitute parent. That's not going to be you.

The Self-Inventory

I'm about to give you some hard work that's so difficult you might find yourself wanting to cry. You'll be pushed out of your comfort zone and asked to make some difficult shifts within yourself and within your family that may not feel good, especially at first. This work is only the beginning as we gather critical information. When you finish these preliminary efforts, even more hard work begins. If I'm scaring you away or you're thinking, "Hold up, my family just needs a little fine tuning, not an onerous transformation," don't throw in the towel just yet or resign yourself to the status quo. The endeavor you're about to take on is the greatest investment you can make for your family; more than any other investment in your life, it will give you the most abundant return you could imagine. And those tears? Some will be tears of frustration, discomfort, disappointment, and fear, but I can guarantee you that most of all there will be tears of joy. It will all be worth it.

Now that you understand why self-awareness is a critical part of your parenting, it's time to uncover and begin to clean up the cobwebs from your past that haunt you or hinder you—and your children. Open your heart and truthfully answer these questions, because it will propel the positive forward. This work is essential to your own healing, for understanding the conditions in which crises emerge, and then for solving problems. The goal is not to start beating yourself up as you get honest with yourself about the past and present. Rather, we must assess where you've been and where you are, because we can't fix problems or circumstances that we're not aware of. So grab a pen and paper, or get to work right in this book.

- **How do you provide your children with physical safety, emotional safety, and permanence?**
- **Are there any factors in their lives, whether in your control or not, that might have led to a disruption in your children's sense of these most fundamental needs?**
- **Do you accept your child for who they are today?**
- **Do you show affection to your child regularly? If so, how?**
- **Do you show your child respect and support their independence?**
- **Do you know your child's friends as well as their hobbies and extracurricular activities?**
- **What do you perceive as your strengths as a parent? What have you done as a parent that felt successful?**
- **What do you perceive as your needs as a parent?**
- **What has been your best learning experience as a parent? If you could get a "do-over" in any aspect of your parenting thus far, what would it be?**

- How do you perform your role as a family manager, the leader of your family unit? Do you share this role with your partner? Who takes the lead in which situations?
- Do you ever feel inadequate or sidelined when it comes to your role as a parent? Have you ever discussed with your caregiving partner how you each handle your roles, or were they taken on by default?
- Do you have the ability to coparent peacefully and effectively with an ex or current partner? If not, what are the biggest obstacles you face in terms of creating a parenting partnership?
- How much of your effort as a caregiver and family manager do your children see you put in? How much of your effort takes place outside of their view?
- Do you ever feel that the pressures or influences of the outside world impact the way you parent? What pulls your attention away or prevents you from acting as a family manager?
- What were the positives and negatives of your childhood? What experiences do you want to emulate? What experiences or patterns do you want to steer far away from?
- Have you explored what factors from your upbringing have made an impact on the way that you parent? What might the baggage you brought from your own family of origin look like?
- Are there things from your childhood and family of origin that you plan to handle differently or do

better? Do you know specifically what you want to change, or are you just going entirely in the opposite direction from how you were raised?

- Can you identify any seeds in your relationship to your family now that could possibly grow to be problems for your family in the future? What might be the underlying reasons for how those seeds got planted? How, if at all, might you have played a role in cultivating them?

- Do you ask yourself consistently, "Is this in the best interests of my child?" Do you distinguish between your own needs and wants and those of your child?

- Do you feel that you have a clear plan of action with your parenting, or are you just shooting from the hip? Do you know your expectations for your family system, and have you clearly articulated them? Do you have a vision and definition of what a successful family system looks like?

- What values are most important to you individually and collectively as a family?

My goal with all of these questions is to help you take a step outside of the immediate circumstances that brought you to this book and start looking objectively at all the factors affecting your ability to create the family life you crave. What's working? What's not working? This isn't about assigning blame; it's about giving you a chance to forecast how the things you're doing today will impact the future, whether good or bad. This work is essential for healing and solving problems. It's nonjudgmental; it's simply crucial to honestly assess the conditions in which crises emerge. We can't fix problems we don't acknowledge, and doing this work is how we can begin to be the parents our kids need and, perhaps, the parents we needed.

By the same token, the changes you make today can alter that forecast for your family as a system and each member as an individual. Learning how today's parenting decisions influence your family's future is critical information. It may inspire you to take a life-changing left-hand turn instead of going straight through that dangerous intersection.

The Child Inventory

It's important that you start this process off by remembering the value that each member of the family brings to the table. So let's begin by making a list of those behaviors your child does well. These are your child's strengths.

- What lights your child up?
- Where do they excel?
- What makes them smile?
- What comes easily to them?
- What do they like to spend their time doing?

Next, let's make a list of those behaviors and attributes you want your child to possess. Do you want them to be more reliable? Do you want them to be better at remembering to do chores and homework without being asked? Do you want them to be tidier and take better care of their space and their things? Do you want them to be kinder, more engaged, more motivated?

Now compare those lists and think about the behaviors you need to master as their primary role model for showing why these skills are important and how to execute them throughout daily life. Focusing on the positive is the only way to make a lasting shift in behavior, along with parental clarity, commitment to the principles, and agreed-upon behavioral outcomes.

These lists of attributes and strengths can be valuable guides as you begin to focus on what's important to you for your family, and what will motivate your child to begin developing the skills they need to thrive.

CHAPTER 3

Understanding Your Baggage

Y ou're beginning to understand how your upbringing made an imprint on who you are as a person and who you are now as a parent. No matter what kind of childhood any of us had, good or bad in your opinion, we are never immune to this imprint. Crystallizing your awareness about aspects of your youth that you appreciated, think missed the mark, or downright abhorred is not an exercise in blaming your parents. Get rid of that mindset or hope if you harbor resentment or are looking for a scapegoat. You had no choice in how you were raised, no choice in how that has programmed you to become the parent you are. Pointing the finger at your parents at this stage serves nobody at all. It's up to you to redirect those parenting outcomes no matter what you came from. It's important to remember that how we deal with the marks our past left on us determines how we excel or fail as parents.

So let's look closer at your self-inventory and begin to assess how your past has affected you. We will explore factors such as your decision making, priorities, and your ability to recognize red flags and empower you to steer your family away from them. Then we will learn how to repack our baggage in ways that allow us to end the cycles from our past that need to be put to rest; maintain aspects that are worth keeping; improve upon some elements; and set our own family up with a new, strong foundation for the future.

Hybrid Parenting

When I was a young adult, it used to drive me crazy when my mother would overreact about anything and everything. This was a regular occurrence. It could be as minor as her calling me for dinner, and if I didn't come in a timely manner, she'd call again and again and again, usually shouting at the top of her lungs with her exasperation palpable throughout the house. This would incite my father to come and get me, which would then lead to us sitting down to the table with tempers flaring. All that just to get me to sit down for dinner! As I matured and after a diagnosis of ADHD, I began to realize that my continuous distraction is what compelled my mother to feel she needed to escalate her behavior to get my attention. Once I got support to focus better and understood why my mom behaved the way she did, we got to a place where neither of us was triggered.

Now, as a parent, I oftentimes find myself frustrated when *my* child doesn't respond on *my* timeline. Because of my upbringing, my initial instinct is to escalate when I don't get the response from him that I want when I want it. But because I have taken an inventory of my past, I know that a cautionary tale from my childhood is that I need to control myself from overreacting. I also am on high alert from letting a fear-based response take hold. Just because I had an underlying reason for my behavior does not mean there is something "wrong" with my son when he doesn't adhere to my timetable. It is just my imprint that triggers me.

This understanding of my origins, what I call unpacking our baggage, helped me help myself, and in turn, my child. I have now repacked my bags as a parent by reframing my perception of my son's behavior and controlling myself from overreacting. I need to walk to where he is and ask nicely, not stir up the whole house to join my crusade until I see movement toward the dining room table. I don't need to overreact to get his attention because I know all too well how that kind of reaction made me feel. So because of what I've been able to *learn* from my upbringing, when he doesn't respond to me, or if he says, "I'll be right there" but I see no sign of that happening, I don't go berserk.

Most nights, we make it to the dinner table in peace, thanks to what I call a hybrid model of parenting. I didn't make a sharp U-turn from how I was raised by letting dinnertime become a come-when-you-feel-like-it free-for-all. Nor did I replicate what my parents did, because I know how that made me feel. I have learned to distinguish between my own limitations as a parent and my son responding to life through a different lens. He can be very in tune with our own family's guiding principles (not that he always is!) and still react to life's circumstances quite differently. And that's okay.

Likewise, you don't need to parent exactly like your parents (no matter how good a job they did), and you shouldn't try to raise your kids in a polar opposite way (no matter how undesirable your childhood was). Your child is not a carbon copy of you, so thinking you can just replicate your parents' strategy doesn't leave enough room to honor your child's individuality. That mindset could, in fact, blind you to their needs and hinder you from modifying your family structure accordingly. On the flip side, doing the exact opposite of what your parents did is not a surefire way of preventing your kids from an experience like yours.

Think about a child whose parents are so strict about sugar that they don't allow any sweets whatsoever. When the child walks by a candy store one day and races inside, you can imagine the lack of restraint he'll exhibit and how the ongoing deprivation will land him precisely where his parents didn't want him to be. Once he sees what he's been missing, he'll crave it even more, and go to great lengths to indulge in this forbidden fruit consistently. The same holds true if you steer your family ever so sharply to whatever direction is furthest from your up-bringing. That's why a hybrid model is so important. You should also make a concerted effort with your partner to find the strengths you each have as parents, maybe strengths you learned from your parents, and create a parenting strategy that combines the best of both of you.

Reframing the Past

Let's dig a little deeper together, right now. Remember, this isn't about playing a blame game. It's about asking yourself some tough questions, holding yourself accountable, and being the best parent you can be, for yourself and for your kids.

- What aspects, if any, from your childhood do you most want to replicate? Why?
- What aspects, if any, from your childhood would you most like to avoid repeating? Why?
- Where is your parenting foundation rooted? Are you parenting in a way that duplicates what your parents did? Are you choosing to parent differently than your parents did? Why? Which of those strategies seem to be working, and which of them are not?

Let's turn to how you respond to poor behavior from your child, because it can be tricky to differentiate if you're reacting to your child in certain moments or being triggered by your own childhood experiences.

- How does it affect you when your child misbehaves? Get specific about how it makes you feel.
- How do you respond to your child when they misbehave? Do you use those moments as teaching opportunities, even if you choose to punish them?
- What behaviors from your child elicit the biggest reactions from you? What is it about those behaviors that really get to you?

No matter who we are, what we do, or whatever work we've done in evolving, we're going to be impacted by repeated patterns from our past until we connect the dots that help us eradicate our response to them. That's not to say that everything your parents did that you took negatively now has a negative impact. Not at all. In fact, when you do your work properly, all of your experiences can be turned into lessons in disguise. For instance, perhaps your family never ate dinner together growing up, and that made you feel sad because you missed out on family time or you were lonely while you ate staring at reruns on TV. It would be expected that you would see that as a negative in your parents' childrearing, a missed opportunity for family bonding, and a choice that may have left you feeling not prioritized. But you can now see that you should try extra hard to make sure *your* family eats together, right? In that sense, it's a good lesson. It taught you that there is an importance to family time and encouraged you to make dinnertime a meaningful touchpoint for you and your children.

Now take a moment to look back and ponder some possible reasons why your parents weren't able to have family dinners. Maybe they didn't have the money to have a proper dinner all together consistently, or perhaps their work schedules made it too difficult to coordinate. Are there explanations for why they didn't parent in a way in which you wanted? How do you feel it affected you? How will you communicate those experiences to your children in a way that can create a positive experience and moment of connection between you? Realize that there are benefits to the positive and the negative.

I'll give another example. I have a patient whose mother was always late to pickup from school when it was her turn to drive carpool. My patient would have to wait in the rain until her mom pulled up in the station wagon, always with a different excuse for the holdup. My patient, who is now a mom, had to do the work to understand what was going on back then. From her perspective as an adult, she became able to appreciate how stretched thin her mom was, and that there simply wasn't enough time after her workday ended to make it crosstown for the pickup on time. Only now can she understand that the fifteen intolerable minutes she waited on a street corner were not the sum total of her overworked mom's love (or lack thereof). She has repacked that baggage to do better for her kids, and you can be darn sure that when the school bell rings, she's standing exactly where her child can see and feel the sense of safety she longed for in her youth.

At the same time, we have also worked on her not having her child's school bell feel like a bomb detonating, as if that that's the precise moment when her love must be at the ready or she has failed. She was just a few minutes late once, and she absolutely fell apart even though her child was completely fine. "Promise me you forgive me and know I still love you!" she implored through tears to her first grader, projecting decades of pain onto an unsuspecting and confused child. This imprint of abandonment that she felt—and continues to feel—can't all be channeled into showing up on time at the end of the school day. Aside from burdening her child with her baggage, she needs to caution herself from becoming so vigilant about that one aspect of her parenting that she neglects to nurture other aspects of her child's safety or develops a blind spot to his other needs. These are complicated emotions that we've worked together to unpack and heal. With a hybrid model of parenting, she reframes her past and repacks her bags so she does better than her own mom did, but not at all costs and without going overboard.

Through a Different Lens

Let's now do an exercise to aid you in acknowledging and confronting your past. You can't change what you've experienced, but you can move forward from it as a stronger, healthier parent to your own children.

- What aspects of your parenting do you question? When do you find yourself second-guessing an action, reaction, or choice?
- What do you believe you are doing successfully as a parent? What are you proud of for doing well and want reinforced?
- What things that you are currently doing in your parenting style do you believe should go in a different direction? What behaviors of yours aren't getting the results that you want?

Your answers to these questions are likely based on the feedback you get from your kids. The lens through which you judge yourself now as a parent is guided by your child's response to your behavior. If your child is really raging against your approach to discipline, for example, that might be an area where you second-guess yourself, perhaps wondering why your rules aren't enforcing the boundaries you want to set. Or you might think you're doing a phenomenal job in exposing your children to culture based on how they have developed a love of theater thanks to you, even though the cost of the tickets is starting to drive up your credit card bill. So as we take a closer look at your own childhood next, let's keep in mind how your priorities as a parent now—whether it's the way you set rules, spend money, or anything else—may be informed by the experiences you had as a child.

You may want to do this next exercise with a sibling if you have one because it can be helpful to see if your memory serves you correctly, or they could jog your memory as you look back in time together. Whether you do it alone or with a sibling, try to remember exactly how you felt when your parents parented as they did. Remember, you may see them differently now that you have your own kids, but try to change the lens on your microscope through which you look at your childhood to remember how you felt back then.

- As a child, what were the strengths you perceived in your mother?
- What were the strengths of your father?
- What were the areas of improvement for your mother?
- What were the areas of improvement for your father?
- My mother's language of love was . . .
- My father's language of love was . . .
- As a child, when you were frightened, who consoled you and how?

- As a child, what made you feel ultimate emotional and physical safety?
- What painful memories still haunt you?
- Was there a time your family was at a breaking point?
- When my parents argued, they would . . .
- What aspects of your mother's style of parenting do you want to avoid as a parent?
- What aspects of your father's style of parenting do you want to avoid as a parent?
- The most resentful feeling I have toward my mother is from . . .
- The most resentful feeling I have toward my father is from . . .
- The relationship with my mother has poisoned my own parenting by . . .
- The relationship with my father has poisoned my own parenting by . . .
- If I were given sixty seconds before I die, I would say to my mother . . .
- If I were given sixty seconds before I die, I would say to my father . . .
- What's a one-word description of your mother's parenting style?
- What's a one-word description of your father's parenting style?
- Who else besides your parents were significant in your childhood and how did they impact your life?
- What similarity do you see between your mother's style of parenting and yours?

- What similarity do you see between your father's style of parenting and yours?
- I would definitely not do _____ as my mother did.
- I would definitely not do _____ as my father did.
- When you argued with your mother, what was the process of reconciliation, if there was one, like?
- When you argued with your father, what was the process of reconciliation, if there was one, like?

This process of going back in time, digging deeply into how you experienced your parents' actions years ago, and writing all these remembrances down is a big part of the unpacking experience. Now let's change the lens on your microscope to think about why your parents may have parented in that way. You're a parent now, and you've got, ostensibly, a very different perspective on their actions and beliefs than you had all those years ago. For each question you answered above, and with each piece of baggage you unpacked, it's time to examine them from your perspective as an adult. Consider the underlying reasons for their parenting style and specific decisions. Some questions to consider as you create a somewhat simplified understanding of your parents' possible motivations: Were they trying to keep peace in the family? Calming everyone down in a moment of discomfort? Placating you when you might have needed it? Doing whatever they did to show their love, even if that's not how you experienced it? Disciplining you harshly because from their perspective you were getting out of control? How did your parents' interaction with each other impact the parenting you received? What dynamics did you observe between the people who were tasked with creating stability for you as a child? Get specific as you try to unpack the origins of their behavior and generate educated hypotheses about the real meaning of what your parents did or didn't do and why.

Along the way, if you find yourself asking, "What am I doing all this for?" then I ask you in return: Do you want to function more optimally as a person, parent, friend, and in any other roles that matter to you? Do you want to hold yourself to high standards while also treating yourself kindly and with compassion? Do you want a strategy to help you stay on track when you feel derailed? How about any changes you'd like to see with your kids: Do you want to develop a more trusting, intimate bond with them? Do you want them to grow up feeling a sense of self-worth that propels them to pursue meaningful careers and build fulfilling relationships? Would you like to watch them seize opportunities with confidence, knowing exactly who they are and where they come from? Do you wish for them to remain whole and grounded when they hit inevitable bumps in the road of life? Let's take it even further and think about your grandkids: Do you want them to live their life to the fullest and look back with the utmost respect for their legacy?

These are just some of the returns on your investment that you'll see starting now and for decades ahead. When you do the work that solidifies your family's foundation and launches all of you into an exponentially better place, then even future generations are beneficiaries of your investment. Before you can see those returns yourself and set up your children and grandchildren to reap the rewards, too, you've got to put in an investment. That investment started when you bought this book and committed to do better for your kids.

You've got to examine your parents' parenting with your adult lens so you can take this exercise to its next step: comparing and contrasting their parenting with how you parent today.

What was happening then, when you were a child, and what is

happening now that you are a parent? What differences and similarities do you see, not just between you and your kids but between you and your partner as well? Be aware of how you're feeling throughout this whole process. If you are reacting strongly in a negative way to something from your childhood, that is a red flag to be explored, because that could drive you to parent in a polar opposite way, reeling against your parents, but *no extreme is good.* If you choose to do exactly what they did or precisely the opposite, you put yourself and your children at risk too. Instead, use your understanding of your parents' reasoning to make more informed decisions. If they were motivated by fear, perhaps an emotion that you now feel at times, how could you channel that fear differently? If they made poor decisions because they didn't understand what you were going through, how will you engage with your child and truly grasp their experience so you can support them more appropriately and wholly?

You have just completed some of the most important housekeeping you'll ever do. You can look at your family and your life with clean lenses, giving you much better vision and clarity. What you see is likely the good, the bad, and the somewhere-in-the-middle about your experiences as a child in a way that can benefit both you and your children. It's a new way of thinking, and it's a way to look in your rearview mirror with understanding, forgiveness, growth, and power. You know where you came from, you have a better understanding of how things are now and what needs to be changed. And now we can start to solidify where you want to go and how to get there. That life-changing lens change and self-awareness is just a start. Throughout the rest of this book I will arm you with tools to help you repack your bags with just what you need to take you and your family to the next level.

CHAPTER 4

Toxic Power Dynamics

M eet Sasha, a twelve-year-old who was brought to me by her parents, John and Elaine. Sasha had two younger siblings, an eight-year-old sister and a five-year-old brother. John was a real estate broker and Elaine a stay-at-home mom who did all the work to keep their family and home afloat as best she could. They came with Sasha to meet with me the day after she was sent home from school for carving "I want to blow this place up and then kill myself" into her desk.

After much investigation and handwriting comparisons, school officials were able to identify Sasha as the author of those terrifying words. When they confronted her, she denied it and began to scream and cry. The school called her parents, asked that she be evaluated, and not returned to school until she was deemed not a threat to herself or others. It often takes a severe wake-up call like that, perhaps involving DCFS, for a family to take off their blinders and get real about what's going on in their own home, under their supposed control.

Until that point, Sasha's parents had no idea that their daughter was silently suffering. And once I met with them, I quickly asked myself, "How would they?" Sasha had her own room at the other end of the house, and she rarely ate dinner with the family, choosing instead to eat alone in her room or not at all. She was able to have her friends over anytime she wanted during the week or on weekends. She had the freedom and the means to buy more designer clothes and handbags than most adults have in a lifetime. She rarely interacted with her siblings or engaged with her parents, and when she did, it was typically a conflict that escalated until profanity was shouted at top volume and doors were slammed.

In response to the incident at school, Sasha and her family had been entered into the system and needed to get help. If you've ever been in the position of getting the call from school, Child Services, the Police Department, or other authority, you know how crushing it can be. I've had parents tell me they feel shame, failure, and profound fear from having their family dynamics suddenly playing out in public. It's a major escalation, and one that needs to be taken seriously. But have you ever heard of silver linings, or the notion that sometimes something good can come out of a situation that starts off feeling really bad? Well, that's the case with Sasha, and with so many of the families who come to me at a moment of crisis.

Nine out of ten times when I saw a family being presented to the child abuse hotline, no matter what their economic status was, their cultural background, racial identity, or any other specific defining characteristic, they were there because they were hitting the wall in some manner. The kids I meet feel bad. I know their parents are almost always petrified. But I also know that if they follow the lead given to them by the child welfare system, sometimes in conjunction with the court, the disruption of having to show up in my office could become a catalyst for much-needed change. We've all heard the phrase "no pain, no gain," and in these cases it couldn't be more accurate. The pain that comes from disrupting a destructive pattern in the family structure, no matter how impossible it seems to overcome and even if outside forces are involved, will pale in comparison to the stability, joy, and overall value that your family will have after the transformation that gets everyone on track. The work isn't easy, but it pays off.

Breaking Through Paralysis

John and Elaine explained to me that they intentionally gave Sasha a room at the other end of the house and never pushed her to sit down for meals or conversation. Instead, they tiptoed around to avoid the chaos they knew would ensue if she joined any family activity. In my time with each of them, both parents revealed to me how they felt: "like prisoners in our own home." The only reason they finally confronted the situation was because Sasha couldn't attend school until she got evaluated by someone like me who could understand what was driving her to want to die, or to carve that into a desk even if she didn't actually feel that way.

I explained to Sasha's parents that the day they started backing away from their daughter in fear of her behavior or just out of avoidance was the day they started to give up their power to her. That, they agreed, was when Sasha was about eight years old. So for approximately four years they had slowly been handing over the reins to a preteen—a preteen with an undeveloped brain, I should add, whose basic needs for safety and permanence were far from being met.

This also diminished any parenting power they may have otherwise had with their two younger children because Sasha was now in charge in their home and was modeling this dangerous parent-child dynamic for all. The more that Sasha was demanding and bullying toward her parents, the more fearful and hopeless they became. Each time they gave up just a little more of their authority and let Sasha run her own show, their tween accumulated more power—until the point came when she had so much power she didn't know what to do with it. It was so overwhelming, paralyzing, and fear-provoking that in her mind, the only option was to die, or at least scream for help with a horrifying threat.

It is overwhelming to face the many problems that are produced from a family that is dysregulated due to a parenting power loss. This dynamic creates so many uncomfortable feelings that I often see parents deny it, ignore it, or explain it away. Unfortunately, this is like putting gas into an already-existing inferno. The longer you wait to address it, the higher the potential for long-lasting damage; therefore, it's imperative that you take charge of this loss of power and do the work on yourself, come together with your parenting partner if you have one, and define the path you'll commit to walking together to regain the power you have lost over time to your children.

Clearly, this family came to my office because of Sasha, who was perceived as the "problem child," or the Identified Patient. She was not the root cause of this family's upheaval or the real patient in the disintegration of a suitable power dynamic between parent and child. The IP is oftentimes healthier than the real patient, who is usually unaware of their role. Yes, I said "healthier" when referring in this case to Sasha, because she was self-aware enough to feel the discomfort and pain that came from overturning the parenting power structure, even if she helped flip it on its head. Her parents, on the other hand, couldn't see the source of the conflict, and responded by further backing away when Sasha's behavior began to devolve. They may have done that in a feeble attempt to regain power, but what actually happened was that they were further bullied, fearful of their child, and handed over their authority on a silver platter.

Erosion of Power

Sasha's story shows us a very common way by which a child steals power from their parents and the parents ignore the power loss, adopting a mindset that as long as their child seems happy, everything will be okay. Again, the parents may have many reasons for subconsciously or consciously surrendering their power, including fear, feeling unloved by their child, or lacking the know-how to use it, but none of those justifications makes it acceptable. Some parents also resort to humor, laughing off an unhealthy and dangerous imbalance of power with lines like "Our little one runs the entire house!" or "There she goes again, bossing everyone around. She's going to make an amazing CEO one day!" Though humor has its place in parenting, which we'll get to in the pages ahead, it's not funny in this context. Far from it. I'm here to tell you that if your child is happy because they've stolen your power, everything won't be okay again until that power—your critical parenting power—is back in your hands. Keep in mind that the problems a child's power grab creates aren't limited to the parent-child dynamics in your home. Just as a child with too much power feels comfortable—even entitled—when bullying parents or siblings, so, too, are they likely to approach relationships at school and beyond with the mindset or actions of a bully. They practice it all too well at home and then take this behavior out into the world. When the appropriate power structure is missing from the home, children lack the self-regulation, boundaries, and respect that are necessary to form peer-to-peer relationships. They resort to trial and error, including bullying, as they painstakingly navigate power dynamics and learn the hard way that their power is not—nor should it be—unrestricted.

But how did that happen to Sasha's family, and to so many of the families that I work with where the power dynamic between parent and child has fallen way out of whack? The erosion of the family power dynamic begins early on. Do you recall the very first moment your baby breathed new life into this world and you became a parent? You probably stared in complete awe at your newborn, in disbelief that you created a human being and now had the awesome responsibility of raising a child as part of your family. It was in that moment that the power dynamic of your family inevitably shifted. That baby arrived with a significant amount of power just by virtue of turning you into a parent (and turning your life upside down, too). From that moment on, the child impacts the family's power dynamic. The misconception here is that the child is the one who throws the preexisting power dynamic out the window, when in fact it's up to the parents to carve out the space and call the shots that have the child fit in to the structures already in play. But here's what goes wrong: Parents are frequently so blinded by love for their child, by wanting to be loved in return, or by fear of doing something wrong that they hand over their power to that child in the years that follow. In some families, the erosion of power stems from a parent who's so committed to doing the opposite of what their own parents did that they don't even recognize their child's ever-growing authority. Their misguided approach to not repeating their own parents' mistakes blinds them to the fact that they are, in essence, becoming subservient to their child.

Even attempts to give a child agency and control over their lives can go too far, sliding away from allowing a child healthy and age-appropriate opportunities to self-express and into a realm where the child feels that they are responsible for all the decision making. This can ultimately cause the child to lose their sense of safety. When this happens, they're off to the races in the power dynamic erosion; a child's conflicted feelings about wanting to get their way versus their sense that nobody is in charge can cause them to try to relieve themselves of the power they should instead be developing with the guidance of a parent who knows their place in the parent-child dynamic.

Many variables from several different perspectives play into this power shift. It may be a mother or a father who is intimidated by their child, or it can be a powerful child who doesn't ever back down (or both). The power shift could stem from one parent feeling left out, typically the nonchildbearing parent who is unsure of their role, and then subconsciously relinquishes their power to the child. Sometimes it's the firstborn who rocks your world more so than any subsequent children do. Or it could be your youngest child, whose arrival shifts the power dynamics so substantially that your family feels like a sinking boat. The permutations of what this power shift can look like are endless, but the strategies for being able to ride the waves with your power intact are consistent.

It's incredibly important to remember that just because a child is able to usurp parental authority and disenfranchise their parents doesn't mean that's what the child wants. It certainly doesn't mean that they know what to do with all that power. In fact, it's for those very reasons that they become the Identified Patient. A child with an inappropriate amount of power, like Sasha, is a recipe for disaster, for themselves and others. Regaining your power as a parent is the single most important thing you can do to reestablish the essentials kids need—safety, permanence, and freedom to be kids. So even though we're just beginning to explore the tools you'll need to actually achieve that goal, commit to doing it right now. In making that commitment, know how laborious the effort you'll need to turn the ship around will be, but it's crucial and even lifesaving.

When Money Is the Power

Let's look at other ways by which a child can steal power, and over time, how the family's structures—and values—decrease all too quickly and severely.

Judith and her husband, Peter, had been married for approximately sixteen years and had four children, ages four to fifteen. Their fifteen-year-old son, Sam, was the IP and the reason that this family came to my attention. Sam, a high school sophomore, hadn't attended his regular school because was under house arrest due to drug possession. In many cases it takes a life-changing or life-threatening event to disrupt the power dynamic that has devolved to such an undesirable level. I guess you could say that, thanks to Sam, that's exactly what happened to this family.

During the summer before his junior year, Sam was staying over at a friend's house one night. They were out late when Sam got arrested for drug possession. His parents had known that he dabbled with alcohol every now and then, and a little weed here and there, but nothing that they thought was interfering with his ability to function at school or at home. Little did they know that Sam had a full-blown addiction, and he was holding his life together just well enough to hide it from his parents.

After his arrest, he was remanded by the court to an inpatient substance-abuse treatment facility, followed by an outpatient program. Family therapy was interwoven in those treatment modalities.

His parents had also started couples therapy to work through the disappointment and internal conflict exacerbated by their son's arrest. When I joined the family's medical team, we further connected the dots of how they had gotten to this place. Once everyone in the family was able to see the patterns that had led them to my office, we came up with a plan together to restore the balance of the family power dynamics.

Sam, Judith and Peter's firstborn, stole the power right from the hands of his parents soon after his birth. Peter can recall almost to the day when he saw the shift happen between him and his wife and between his wife and their son. There was a distinct moment when Peter noticed that he had slipped into third position in his family and no longer felt that he was being treated as an equal parenting partner or respected husband. It was just over a cup of coffee, but it was profound. Judith and Peter had always enjoyed their morning ritual together, but there came a time when Judith was so focused on Sam that their cherished husband-and-wife time evaporated.

Over the next fifteen years, the power continued to shift in Sam's direction. Judith and Peter had three other children, none of whom had the same kind of power that Sam had, especially over his mother. Judith would go to extraordinary measures to make sure that Sam didn't feel the pain of any consequences of his behavior or suffer in any way when he didn't comply with the expectations or rules that applied to the rest of his family. For instance, the entire family might be sitting down to dinner and just have to wait and wait until Sam finally decided he was ready to heed the multiple calls to come to the table. Rather than have an allowance, Sam went to his mom whenever he wanted anything, and she gave him the money he asked for. Peter and Judith fought over why she continued to enable Sam to run their home with his behavior, avoidance, and disrespect for either of their directives, but the unhealthy dynamics became more and more entrenched.

There are many poisonous elements that feed the beast inside a child who has stolen parental power, and money is one of the most damaging. Judith fooled herself into thinking that giving Sam money was an act of love. Even if he hadn't used the money for drugs—which he did—it was a destructive parenting move. Ever heard the saying "Money talks"? What that money translates to is power. The minute it's in your child's hands, that's what they feel. And if they have not learned how to manage that money, if they have not been given boundaries, budgets, or had the lived experience of earning money in a way that deeply allows them to understand the value of the work that goes into making money, they will have absolutely no ability or desire to ever handle money responsibly. Money gives them the ability to do what they want, and that's dangerous when the power is beyond what their brain is capable of processing.

Brain development cannot be rushed or bypassed, even if your child is mature and responsible most of the time. Giving your child too much money or regular access to money before their brain is developed enough to have impulse control, judgment, and insight is like giving your car keys to a ten-year-old and encouraging them to take the car for a spin. In my many years of experience with disparate populations and family structures, I can tell you that families that show love with money are among the most difficult power shifts to fix.

But fixing it is precisely what we can and will do. By identifying the parenting power loss and modifying the dysregulation through rebalancing—ideally before you reach the breaking point that could have the child welfare system knocking at your door—you'll put out the fire that is burning down your house. Even if it's an inferno that's blazing, we will put the structure back in place and restore the power that you must have to increase your family's value. It's never too late. You owe it to your child before you send them out into the world with a false or inappropriate sense of power that will, at best, not serve them well and, at worst, lead them to crash and burn, taking all of you along for the ride.

Taking the Power Back

When I sit down with families early on in our work together, I ask them to take a "Family Power Questionnaire" to help me understand where they are now, or at least their perception of where they are. This is work that can be uncomfortable, but remember: This isn't about assigning blame. Parents need to have an honest and accurate understanding of what's happening in the family, and too often I meet with families who are so overwhelmed that they don't even have a clear sense of the factors that are contributing to the chaos. In order to establish boundaries, trust, and communication, families need to understand what their baseline is. So I now ask you to do the same.

Family Power Questionnaire

You'll notice as you go through these questions that I'm asking about *you*, not about whether your child tries to boss you around, how they respond to your discipline (or lack thereof), or what kind of shouting matches may be happening under your roof when heads butt. If that's the case, you lost your power some time ago. These questions are about you because the goal is to awaken the feelings you may have around your child that are leading you to back away or contributing to a dysregulated power dynamic. If you answer yes to any one of the following questions, consider it a red flag for parental power loss:

- Do you find yourself getting increasingly angry when responding to your child?
- Do you feel you are trying to exert control over your child when disciplining?
- Do you find a loss of words or focus when responding to your child?
- Do you feel your responses to your child are often more ambiguous than they should be?
- Do you find yourself stumbling, hesitating, or feeling insecure when responding to your child?
- Have you noticed if your responses to your child are becoming increasingly threatening or bully-like?

With Sasha's family, it was abundantly clear that parental power loss had already reached an untenable place and that the dynamics needed a transformation. We started by having a first-ever family meeting to let the kids know that the way business will be conducted in their home going forward was about to change. This was the beginning of the shifting of power back into the hands of her parents. I'm all for transparency and spelling it out for the kids so there are no surprises, including how the family arrived at this place of needing realignment. I understand that it's not easy for parents to initiate a dialogue that's essentially telling the kids that their destructive party is coming to an end. Those uncomfortable feelings are just an indication that both the conversation and the change are imperative.

Then we had every member of Sasha's family do an assessment to evaluate five critical aspects of their well-being (you'll learn how to do this assessment in your own life later in this book), because power struggles aren't really just about whether a teen defies a curfew or who calls the shots at a particular moment in time. There are underlying causes, and we need to address them at the most baseline level—starting with, for example, sleep. Because Sasha's assessment showed that her sleep was erratic and unstructured, she was placed on a daily schedule with a nightly bedtime, as was her entire family. As well, her parents met with school administrators and teachers to address her decompensating academics and social problems with peers, none of which they had been aware of until the wake-up call. They came up with a plan to support her and created some new school responsibilities for her that placed her within a new peer group. Sasha's parents also restructured the mealtime schedule to accommodate as many family members as possible eating together at each meal, ensuring that Sasha was present for at least one each day. Sasha started individual psychotherapy to better understand herself and how to communicate her feelings. At the same time, her family began family therapy to work on the connections among all of them and to learn how to rebound. Sasha's bedroom moved closer to other family members for her to feel part of the family physically, and we worked on improving her confidence and self-esteem by having her choose a team sport.

Now, to be clear: It wasn't easy for Sasha's parents, Elaine and John, to begin this dialogue; that's to be expected. When your child has been running the power dynamic for a while, it is very common for parents to feel intimidated, uncomfortable, or fearful of their child's reaction and the work ahead. So before the family meeting, we talked through strategies that would make the conversation go as smoothly as possible. Elaine and John took my advice and used a whiteboard to prepare their dialogue as a team so they would know who would say what and how they would discuss their family's strengths, not just their weaknesses and shortcomings. Rather than singling out Sasha specifically, they mostly talked about the family unit as a whole so she would feel less defensive. They took a collaborative approach, not an adversarial one.

It may be obvious, but I need to tell you that most members of your family—especially the power stealer—aren't going to react well to the power shift you'll be initiating. You will witness various extremes of resistance and even rebellious behavior. The magnitude of this defiance is directly related to the amount of power that has been usurped from you by your child. In other words, the more resistance, the more power that needs to be regained by you.

One of the biggest reasons why many parents fail at this process, at least initially, is because of how uncomfortable they feel changing the dynamics to which they've grown accustomed, no matter how inappropriate they were. When parents fight, disagree, or can't support each other when one person feels discouraged, it's all too easy to let the toxic dynamics take hold once again. Change is hard! But trust me: Over time it becomes more comfortable, so please don't lose faith when it feels like the uphill climb is too arduous. If you have a coparent, you'll need to support each other when one of you feels weak. The more committed you are to this process, the higher your chances of achieving your desired outcome: taking the power back that will increase your family value.

If your kids say "What the hell is happening here?" or "Are you guys out of your mind?" stay calm when you respond. Let them know that yes, you're well aware that there's a new standard for behavior in the family, and yes, you do believe that each member of the family is capable of adhering to it. Be clear that nobody is expecting perfection, but everyone is expected to make an effort. The more unkindly your children react to the changes, the more you should feel you're on the right path. Pushback and big outbursts from your kids mean they want to keep the power dynamic the way they're used to. But remember that that old model wasn't actually a place of comfort; it was an unhealthy evolution that placed your family at risk.

As for Judith and Peter's family, after the parents worked to get on the same page about the need for change and behaving like the parents they both needed to be, the younger children were pleasantly surprised to have more structure and attention. Sam's reaction to the power shift was quite different. His tantrums escalated, his bullying was magnified, and he downright refused to participate in his family under these new circumstances. They reached a crossroads that many families hit: to continue on the path despite the pushback or to give up and return to their old ways. Judith and Peter pulled together to counter Sam's resistance with consistency in both their behavior and actions. That's not to say that Sam wasn't disgruntled; he surely was. But within about six weeks, he was much more engaged with his family and in a much healthier place. Both of his parents had the power back that they had lost, and all four children felt the safety and permanence they had needed all along. Within four to six months after we met, both Judith and Peter were able to reflect on the differences they saw in their parenting from before the shift and after, and they were very satisfied by the obvious increase in their family values.

There are days when you will feel that the power struggle continues between you and your children similar to a tug-of-war. But those are the days and the times when you need to buckle down, connect tightly with your parenting partner, and get through one minute and one situation at a time. I want to caution you from screaming and yelling as a way to assert your newfound authority. It may take a little time to get comfortable with what your appropriate parental authority feels like, but the goal is for you to remain consistent with the rules and calm in your reinforcement. Having a big emotional reaction to your child's resistance—if you yell, cry, or crumble—is not what power sounds or looks like. In fact, responding to your child from that kind of emotional place is likely how you lost power.

More than likely, there will still be times when your children catch you off guard and you both revert to the old style. That's bound to happen; equally likely is that you and your parenting partner will have days where it's easier or harder to stick with the new plan, and you both will likely find yourselves slipping into old patterns. When that happens, kids will usually do their best to try to split parenting power down the middle; they will wait until they can get one of you alone, they will tell you the other parent gave them permission and they're just seeking your permission as well, and you may fall into that trap. If that happens, don't be hard on yourself. Instead, take it as an opportunity to remind yourself of the goal, check in on yourself to make sure you have your own needs met to allow you to be the parent you want to be, and then use your new parenting tools to reinforce the new standards that your child needs to meet.

Each and every time you don't fall into the trap and handle it in that strategic manner, you're getting further away from the patterns of the past and sending a message to your child that you have control of yourself and the situation. Even though they may feel they got one by you, it's one more behavioral demonstration to them that you're aware of it and shutting it down. This message is important and impactful.

Boundaries for All Ages

In both of these cases, with Sasha and Sam as the Identified Patients, boundaries were a critical part of the solution. All parents must set boundaries. Think of a boundary as the line you draw around yourself that your child is not only aware of but also knows the meaning of that line. This boundary sends the message to your child of where you end and they begin, which sets the standard for where your child's behavior crosses over from acceptable to unacceptable. They need to know that no means no, that yes means yes, and that maybe is nonexistent because you are decisive and stick to your word. Boundaries work best when they are set as early as possible with as much clarity as possible. They also need to have associated consequences that are clearly spelled out and understood by your child. Depending on the age of your child, having them involved in the construction of the consequences can be beneficial. The ultimate key to making boundaries work is you as the parent being as consistent as humanly possible in upholding those boundaries and enforcing those consequences. Each time you lose the consistency of practice of the boundary, you lose power as a parent in the eyes of your child.

A specific boundary might include setting a curfew for your teen, for example. Start by setting a time that works best for you as the parent, taking everyone else's schedule into account. If you need to be asleep by 10:00 p.m., then having your teen home by 9:30 p.m. is appropriate. Make it work for you and the family unit, not just for your teen. This process of setting a curfew is also an opportunity to strengthen collaboration between you and your teen as you explain that your job is to ensure the safety of your whole family, and it's their job to adhere to the rules and show respect for your boundaries. Discuss with your child the trust you're placing in them by allowing them to manage themselves during a specific time frame, and what is expected in return is that they adhere to the boundary of being home by a certain time. Set it up in advance that you'll be more flexible on special occasions, such as a school event, as long as it's discussed ahead of time. Showing that you're open-minded and reasonable goes a long way toward keeping your parenting pattern and your respect. You might consider signing a curfew contract so that nothing is left ambiguous. In that contract, you might elucidate the consequences of being even a few minutes past curfew. Also be sure to use this opportunity to discuss safety and that you would rather them be late than unsafe.

If you're feeling defeated by how substantially your child has undermined your parenting, remember that it took years to get to this place of dysregulation, and it will take time to get out of that dynamic too. When you or your child slip into the patterns that you're trying to eradicate, show them that it doesn't rock your core as it used to. You are in charge now and you'll soon be well equipped to handle bumps in the road. Those bumps will smooth out much more quickly if your response in behavior outweighs your response in words. Hold your ground in a measured and consistent way, reclaiming your power and staying within your newfound role. Success comes when you can consistently practice this new style despite whatever uncomfortable feelings arise within you or your child. These are the times when you must dig deep within yourself or help your parenting partner utilize tools such as empathy, respect, and self-control in your response to your child's desire to keep the power.

When temperatures rise as you all adjust to the new roles in your home, take a step back and check in with both your head and heart as you steer the power dynamics toward their proper places. At various points throughout this journey to reclaim your power, both rationally and emotionally you should have clarity about why you need to be the leader of your family and what that should look like. You're the parent, and you're about to be an even better parent as you fulfill the most important role you'll ever have with the right amount of power to have your children feel the safety and permanence they're screaming for. So listen to both your head and heart as you redefine and reorganize the power differentials and structures within your own home. With every new conversation or incident when you hold your ground and stick to your new plan, you will start to see and feel the shift within your family.

There's nothing better than the day when you and your partner have pushed through, feel exhausted, but can recognize that your children are interacting with you, and with each other, in a different way. Even if it's for five minutes of the day at first, that's a win. You look up at your parenting partner and feel that sense of satisfaction and pride that the shift is happening and that's the motivation to continue supporting each other in this important work with consistency, stamina, and commitment. Each day gets shorter as far as the power struggle and each day gets longer as far as the healthy dynamics and the increase in your family's value.

CHAPTER 5

Taking Stock of Your Parenting Style

Thomas and Aiden had a good father-son relationship until it came to school. Thomas was always on Aiden, fourteen, about his grades and his assignments, pushing him to excel. One night, Thomas checked in later than usual to discover that Aiden still hadn't done his homework. It was too late at night for him to have the wherewithal and time to get it done. The fight of all fights ensued, with screaming, accusations, and name-calling until Aiden stormed out of the house. He had done this before and returned immediately, so Thomas let him go, thinking he would cool off and come back. But this time was different. After half an hour, Thomas went out into the neighborhood to search for his son in the dark. But there was no sign of Aiden. After two hours, Thomas had no choice but to call the police. They found Aiden, brought him home, and then proceeded to involve Child Protective Services, because such cross-reporting is protocol when children are involved to ensure safety and permanence for that child and any other minors in the home. What started as a typical fight between a father and teenage son about getting homework done in a timely manner, about the father wanting his son to fulfill his responsibilities, ended with sirens . . . and my having to step in.

Here's what I uncovered. Thomas, the dad, was a late bloomer when it came to excelling academically. He had pulled himself together just in time to get good enough grades and gain acceptance into a decent college, but from there he still had an uphill battle, not believing in himself, worrying that he would just get by in life by the skin of his teeth, and often beating himself up for not having tried harder, earlier. Even though Thomas graduated and landed a steady job, he had a deep fear that his son wouldn't. He projected his unresolved issues onto Aiden, who didn't understand where his father's reactions were coming from, and interpreted them as a lack of support and confidence in him. The cycle persisted because every time Thomas was triggered by his son, reliving his own missteps as a poor student, he saw in his offspring what he didn't like about *himself*, and these unresolved issues about his own bad habits led him to take his anger out on Aiden. The gap between father and son widened, and their trust, understanding, and communication withered away.

This case illustrates the importance of taking stock of our own baggage because how we bring it to our parenting style has significant implications. If Thomas had had clarity about why he was triggered when he perceived that Aiden was falling short, then Aiden would not have been subjected to the trauma—yes, it's trauma—that ensued. The fighting, the police, the call to Child Protective Services, and the aftermath unnecessarily impacted Aiden's brain development. That's precisely what trauma does on an undeveloped brain, which all teenage brains are. Any event in a child's life that leaves them feeling immediate fear or a threat to their safety can leave a neurological imprint in their evolving brain wiring. The feeling that there could be danger or potential violence, for example, is often perceived as life-threatening to a young brain, which can have lasting effects that manifest in changes to a child's daily routine or atypical reactions to typical life events.

My work with Thomas and Aiden is a reminder that if you find yourself caught in the same toxic loop with your child, it's worth considering if there is an unresolved issue for *you* at play in your parenting. The more you understand yourself and have control over your emotional and mental state, the better you will stay connected with your child.

I also mention this case because it can help us understand different parenting styles, which is what this chapter is about. Thomas lost control of himself, which resulted in Aiden leaving the house. Aiden didn't come back, in part because he felt the lack of control his father had on his own emotions. After a parent gives up control and their child senses it, it typically leads to the parent backtracking, explaining themselves, and in effect asking their child for control back. Bottom line, Thomas was no longer providing the physical or emotional safety that Aiden needed. Aiden had become afraid of his father, and his home was no longer a place of permanence or stability.

Moments like this can be detrimental to the parent-child dynamic because no child should fear their parent. Respect? Yes. Respond to the appropriate delivery of authority, sometimes uncomfortably because a little tension is to be expected at times? Yes. Fear? No. Ideally, Thomas would have had insight about his baggage, and been able to take a step back when he felt triggered. It's as simple as saying, "We are both angry right now and are not communicating productively. Let's take some time, and when you're ready we can talk this through." Acting in this way shows your child not only that you have control of the situation and want to resolve it but also that you respect them, and when children feel a level of respect from their parents, they want to honor it. If Thomas had acted in this way, he would have behaved as a Balanced Parent, which is one of the types of parenting styles we'll now delve into, the kind we should all aspire to be.

Your Parenting Dashboard

Think of your parenting as a dashboard where there are three different dials, each corresponding to a style. When you understand why each of these styles exists, you'll gain a clearer insight into your own parenting. You may see parts of yourself in the descriptions as well as parts of your own parents. It's important to read about the impact that these different styles can have on a family so you can begin to recognize the patterns that have shaped the relationship you have with your children, and how to utilize each style to improve how you parent. Then you'll be able to make the appropriate changes with an understanding of what's to gain, what's at stake, and why. The magic formula of parenting, the one that leads to the best connection with your child as well as the consistency and grounding they need, entails turning the right dials at the right times. When you have each dial in just the right position, not too much of one style or the other, that's when you become a Balanced Parent, which is where our children want and need us to be.

Some of these styles can create tension and imbalance in a family, to a dangerous degree if not checked, so pay attention to possible danger zones. If this breakdown of different types of parents incites you to realize that you've been parenting from an imbalanced position, it's not too late to course-correct. That's precisely why we're looking at these broad types and then going to adjust each dial on that parenting dashboard until the appropriate style takes hold. It's a lifelong pursuit as a parent, not a one-time thing, as you continually modify the imaginary knobs, keep yourself in check, and work to be the best parent you can be at different times in your life and throughout your child's evolving journey. You'll want to consider your own parenting style here, but ideally also work with your co-parent as you uncover how each of you typically parent, and how the combination of your approaches is working—or not.

The Tyrant Parent

Just because I'm using a harsh word such as "tyrant" doesn't mean this kind of parenting style is all bad, because it's not! The Tyrant Parent holds tightly to one set of rules and guidelines regardless of the situation. They lack flexibility, leaving children feeling like they have no voice or ability to create any wiggle room in their parents' decision making, no matter the child's feelings or the unique circumstances.

Being a Tyrant Parent can be effective at times, especially because children seek boundaries, and with a Tyrant Parent the child is never left guessing about where those much-needed guardrails sit. I have one patient whose bedtime regimen is a complete and utter disaster, so we are working on having her turn up the Tyrant Parent dial on her dashboard significantly. My patient was afraid of setting and adhering to hard-and-fast rules because she's running away from the rigidity she abhorred as a child. But as I have said, if we overcorrect in response to our baggage, we run the risk of landing right back where we don't want to be, or worse. In this case, chaos has taken hold, and the inmates are running the asylum as her young children disregard—even mock—her halfhearted attempts to get them in bed. This is just one illustration of how we need aspects of each parenting type at different times, and we've got to understand what lies behind each archetype, or in this case, one's reluctance to dial it up.

Let's look closer at why a Tyrant Parent may behave the way they do. They grab on to the structure and regulations they create, typically to cope with their own unresolved issues. For example, I work with a family that values pedigree above all else. That's not a judgment from me, just a fact that to the head of family, success is defined by a degree from Harvard, Stanford, or the like, period. When summertime comes and other kids enjoy downtime, camp, or leisure activities, this family's children are enrolled in competitive academic and cultural programs intended to bolster their college applications in the years to come, including the fourth grader's. It's never too early and it's never enough because the domineering, accomplished father was denied the opportunity to learn any other metric for measuring one's worth. You are what you accomplish. You are only as good as your last report card. Your college degree defines you for life. Your profession and its prestige are an inextricable part of your identity and value. Any missteps could take you off course, and since there is only one course, in his mind, that could be a consequential mistake. These are just some of the messages that the father had hammered home all of his life, and now he was instilling in his kids. It's complicated, because he's not even sure if that's what he truly wants for them or if he's just so darn angry about his limited life choices that he's taking it out on his kids. Either way, we are working on keeping his Tyrant Parenting in check because those kids deserve room to achieve success beyond that limited definition and not to be burdened by his unyielding expectations.

Not all Tyrant Parents realize they are one. So step one is recognizing your harmful patterns and then step two is addressing them. Something you *must* realize at this moment is that no matter how similar your child's upbringing is to your own, and no matter how much people tell you "the apple doesn't fall far from the tree" because you and your child are so similar, they are having their own experience. They are not necessarily feeling the same way that you felt, and they are not necessarily going to do the things you did, good or bad. Take a step back and ask yourself, "Am I projecting my experiences onto my child? Do I see them for who they really are or for who I want them to be? And where is what I want for them coming from anyway?" Your child isn't you, and deserves the right to experience things in their own ways and be their true selves without the burden of your demons weighing them down.

The next time you feel triggered and respond with harshness or rigidity, I suggest you "unhook and take a look." Acknowledge that you may be acting out on your children because of how you feel about yourself. It's a pretty safe bet that it's connected to your own fears or insufficiencies, and an even surer bet that your tyrannical ways, no matter how well intended, will push your child away and shut them down.

If you feel like you're in a situation that calls for Tyrant Parenting, take a bit of distance to examine what's really going on. Where are your feelings about your current situation coming from? Where did you get the information that is making this situation a crisis? Do you have a complete picture of the immediate circumstances? Is prior baggage taking center stage where it doesn't belong? What is going on with your child, and how many calm conversations have you been able to have with them to get to the bottom of their behavior? If you engage the Tyrant Parent before you have a complete picture of what's going on with you both you and your child, you risk a loss of power and authority as a parent. You also risk your child responding to your half-informed reaction with something along the lines of, "You don't even know about x, y, and z in this situation!"

After you understand how your experience is shaping your perception of your child and you do your due diligence about what you're feeling, why, and what's going on in the situation at hand, you can initiate an honest, impactful discussion. Instead of clinging to rules that may not be serving anyone other than keeping your own anxiety at bay, a better approach would be to engage with your child to find a productive and progressive way toward a solution. The end result of all this work may still involve enforcing a rule or set of consequences. Children do need those! But it will also result in a boundary being strengthened in a healthy, informed way. When your Tyrant is kept in check, you'll be in a much better position to respond in a way that reinforces your family's defining principles rather than further isolating you from your child. You'll use discipline to send a message to your child that you're making well-informed decisions, that you're not just projecting your own unfinished childhood business or having a bad day that you take out on them. You're respecting them and you're parenting them, which sometimes involves appropriate consequences and just the right amount of Tyrant Parenting.

The Feather Parent

On the other end of the spectrum is the Feather Parent. If that's your parenting style, then more often than not you are nonoperational and passive. The Feather Parent may mean well but is ineffective in carrying through with discipline, structure, rules, as well as giving consistent love. That's not to say that a Feather Parent doesn't care about their child; the fact is that they probably very much want their child to be happy and are reacting to a lack of happiness in their own past. But parenting with too light a touch does not help drive children forward toward success, nor does it give them feelings of safety and permanence. Sure, if you're a Feather Parent you aren't screaming, yelling, and instilling fear in your child, and that means something. But, like a feather, you're a weightless influence floating in the air looking pretty and soft. More often than not, you aren't providing the effective parenting children crave or instilling in your children the boundaries they need to feel cared for. If your child just hears noise when you speak instead of listening with the respect a parent deserves, then I question both how you are conveying your messaging and what they may be absorbing instead. If you are Feather Parenting and there isn't already a lack of respect, it's highly likely there will be down the road as your kids gain clarity about what they can get away with and just how ineffective you are as a parent. If you are passive and mean, there is a high likelihood that your child will respond by being very disrespectful and dismissive. If you are passive and nice, you will be treated as a pushover, and the roles in your family will get muddy. Remember, children may act like they want to be in charge and get their way, but they actually need boundaries and consequences to feel safe.

If this is your style, I urge you to think about why. What is going on for you that compels you to Feather Parent? Are you afraid your kids won't like you if you buckle down with discipline? If you hold fast to your word? Were your parents so intense that you struggled to have a positive relationship with them and now you're doing that U-turn that we know isn't the answer either? Are you responding in reaction to your spouse who can be tyrannical? Could it be laziness because implementing consequences requires follow-through, and you just can't muster the bandwidth for that? Some Feather Parents are in such a state of powerlessness that they don't even think about what their child is asking before they automatically respond "Yes." Is that you? If you can understand your motivation for being a Feather Parent and can catch yourself in moments when you know full well that taking a stand and conveying it firmly to your kids are the right things to do, then you'll be able to start getting more comfortable with toughening up your feathers.

One of my patients is a Feather Parent in nearly every realm. She tried getting her kids to do chores so they would develop a sense of responsibility and so that each family member from the youngest to the oldest contributed to the family structure. After one day of bed making and clearing the table, the kids lost interest, and she neglected to follow through. She tried instilling rules for screen time: no iPads or TV until each child had finished homework and thirty minutes of reading. By the end of week they disregarded that directive, knowing full well their mom wouldn't monitor their reading. When she saw that the kids were loading up on too much sugar, she tried implementing a weekends-only policy for dessert. Each Monday they were still eating ice cream sundaes. Her kids knew to expect the same pattern of inconsistency, so much so that they had stopped the charade of even pretending to listen. They knew they would be able to do as they pleased. But at the end of the day, they were left longing for a parent whose word they could trust, who followed through, and who provided predictable, reasonable structures to help them navigate life.

It's not just in the realm of discipline where Feather Parenting can be troublesome. On the afternoon of a birthday party, nine-year-old Helen wanted her beautiful party dress to be wrinkle-free. When she asked her parents if she could try ironing it herself, they acquiesced. Not for one moment did it click for them that she may not have the neuromuscular skills, the brain development, or even the physical strength to deal with an ironing board and a burning hot iron. Quite the contrary. They appreciated her enthusiasm at such a young age to try something new and saw no reason to say no to their self-starting little girl who longed for a perfectly pressed gown. Within minutes of Helen going upstairs to iron her own dress, she was screaming bloody murder and lying under the ironing board with the scalding iron flat on her chest. Nine-year-olds need supervision, instruction, and age-appropriate tasks—it's important to foster their independence, but at all times it's the parents' job to evaluate the safety and responsibility of their child's activities.

Like all parenting types, there are times when Feather Parenting is called for. When your child is making a big life decision that will help them discover their most productive selves, you may want to intentionally take a more passive role to give your child space, as opposed to weighing in heavily with your opinion or bulldozing them with your own expectations. In instances when your child needs to struggle to grow and mature, they may need you to observe instead of react, to give them a chance to be themselves fully. Sometimes you might strategically use a lighter touch as a Feather Parent because it will lead your child in a better direction if they think they're in the driver's seat, when in fact you're behind the wheel, guiding ever so gently. If your child is exceptionally hard on themselves, they might need the reassurance that a Feather Parent offers over the finger wagging of a Tyrant Parent. I saw a middle school young lady who lost her first iPhone within days of this expensive rite of passage being given to her as a birthday gift. Her mom had the incredible foresight to dial up her Feather Parenting when her daughter was beating herself up and devastated about a mistake that she knew wouldn't happen again any time soon, with or without admonishment from her. It was a powerful teaching moment about responsibility, about mistakes, about forgiving oneself.

That moment called for a Feather Parent and nothing more. Turn the Feather Parent dial up when you want your child to feel ultimate security they can be trusted to make their own solid choices, and when you want them to experience ultimate vulnerability as they develop their independence.

The Seesaw Parent

This is a parent who is either indecisive or "seesaws" unpredictably between extremes. The Seesaw Parent seems (and might in fact be) unstable because of the inconsistent presentation of their parenting. There is no consistent reasoning or predictability when it comes to which parenting style gets turned up at what time. They create an environment of confusion for the child which, if not addressed, leads to the child totally disregarding the parent or living in fear because they're so unsure which parenting style will dominate in any particular situation. This parent may be irritated one day, and as a result tell the kids that there is a severe restriction on video games in the house to two hours a week. All of a sudden, with no warning to the kids or even anything they're aware of that provoked this directive, just because the parent is discontented, a rule is instituted. That same parent, maybe during the next week when things are going better for them or just because it strikes their fancy, will say something to the effect of "As long as your work is done, you can play video games all night. Have fun!"

The child sees this inconsistency and starts to distrust that the parent has everything under control. Never knowing what to expect, the child internalizes this unpredictability, suffers from anxiety, and feels especially helpless because they do not understand their role, if any, in the random hand of cards they're dealt. One day this parent could be completely docile, and the next they could be filled with anger. We know how important a sense of safety is for a child; you don't need an MD to see that these extremes are not working toward that purpose and that the stable and predictable guardrails that kids need are lacking with a Seesaw Parent. This lack of safety will have emotional implications for children. They will very likely be untrusting of whomever they have relationships with, and not trust themselves either. Just as you might feel on a seesaw that pulls you down to the ground and then throws you high up in the air—except far worse, because you never know when it's coming—Seesaw Parenting leaves children feeling dizzy and confused, which leads them to feel angry and out of control. When they try to take control, they may be perceived as acting out, when in fact it's a strength that they were able to recognize how they're feeling and try to manage the uncertainty and unpredictability of their situation because they're not getting what they need from their Seesaw Parent.

Seesawing can happen when parents are trying to find their balance. The Feather Parent and Tyrant Parent dials can be sensitive, especially as you are learning how to use them both when different parenting situations call for different styles. The best thing to do is think about regulating your responses. On a scale of one to ten, try to keep your dials between four and six. and let that be the foundation of how you use these tools.

Becoming the Balanced Parent

We all have a duality within us, containing everything we need to set standards and relate with love to our children. If you're aware of it and in control of your varying impulses and strategies, you can reconcile the different facets within yourself and use them to parent well. That's when you become a Balanced Parent. If your fifteen-year-old wants to go out to an unchaperoned party late at night, there is likely one side of you that says "not a chance" and another side that says "it's part of growing up." That's completely normal. You may be worried about their safety, but if you say no immediately, you'll push them away, to possibly more unsafe situations. You child should be aware that you're trying to reconcile the multiple sides, and by trusting them with your thought process you will start a whole new level of trust between you and your child. Mutual respect goes a long way. Lead a discussion with your child, a discussion in which you can be open about your feelings of duality. You can listen and support their reasons for wanting to step outside of your comfort zone without being a pushover. You can express concerns and set parameters without your child hating you. That's what a Balanced Parent does.

You may remember your own parents' cluttered, unkempt house and have an instinct to scream at your kids when they leave their wet towels on the floor or have dog-eared papers covering their desk. I'm all for teaching them a sense of responsibility, but not with a full-time Tyrant Parent who still needs to do their own homework about why untidiness elicits such a big reaction. You may give your child tremendous freedoms because you trust their judgment implicitly, but then don't be shocked when your Feather Parenting lands them in rehab because they desperately needed boundaries and someone to say "no." You need to learn to put away your childhood baggage and separate the immediate information about your child and the situation at hand.

The Balanced Parent is one who can use both ends of the parenting spectrum strategically rather than reactively. This is the parent who knows how to take stock of the situation in front of them and use different parts of their parenting brain depending on what will elicit the most political and productive response at a given moment. It's the parent who allows themselves to "feather" to read a situation and get the most truthful thoughts and feelings out of their child. It's the parent who can then enact the attributes of the good "tyrant," exhibiting that they're the authority, that their children are safe with them as caretakers, and that predictable consequences will be tied to certain behaviors.

No parent is perfect, nor should they strive to be, but everyone can learn to control the dial in each parenting style to become a Balanced Parent. You need to be responsive to your child's needs, recognize your own limitations or preconceived notions, and prioritize providing safety and care while nurturing the child/parent relationship. That's a tall order, but a Balanced Parent, more often than not, has an open dialogue with themselves and with their kids so there's ongoing respect, vulnerability, discussion, and trust. Now, that's a recipe for safety and a foundation to thrive!

PART II

Family Values in Action

CHAPTER 6

SWEEP

Nobody gives you a scorecard to determine how well you're living life. And even if it existed, what would we measure and with what yardstick? How much money you make or when you got your last promotion? If you kept your New Year's resolutions? If you make your bed, walk ten thousand steps daily, have your dream job, or get elected to the head of the PTA? There is no such thing as a grown-up report card, and there are countless ways by which we each evaluate how well we're doing.

While I don't know how you personally measure your overall well-being or success, as a doctor and parent I've created my own tried-and-true assessment tool that applies to all of us. This is the assessment tool I mentioned earlier in the book that worked with Sasha and Sam. You might have heard me talk about it before on *Dr. Phil* or on various podcasts and the like. It's a way to assess how well you're functioning overall based on five key areas of your life that cover the basics of what each of us needs before we can thrive. It's quick and easy enough that you can do it regularly, whether it's daily, weekly, monthly, or even hourly if you'd like. (I'm not so sure your answers will change on an hourly basis, but that's how straightforward it is.) You'll want to do this for yourself as an individual, for your spouse or partner if you have one, for each of your children as individuals, and for your family as a whole.

The Sophy Method is a collection of tools that will give you the vital information you need to understand yourself, your partner, and your family. The Sophy Method is my strategy for assessing where you are today, pinpointing what needs fixing, and then figuring out where you want to end up. This method, which I will teach you throughout the book, involves taking an inventory of your own patterns and habits, looking back at your personal history to identify how themes from your past are impacting the present, and strategies for establishing a structured new set of parameters that will clearly define expectations for the whole family. You can use the Sophy Method for kids of all ages, and it will give you the clarity and confidence you need to be the parent you want your kids to have. With the Sophy Method as your guide, you'll construct a plan to help your family arrive at the outcomes you've agreed upon for increasing your family's value.

There may be a lot of information we need to gather, but there's a simple process I've designed to give you the solid foundation you need to get the results you want. This two-step process entails (1) assessing how well your basic needs are being met, and (2) making a plan to fulfill those needs. The end result will keep you and your family on track toward reaching your goals of knowing what your family truly values and increasing your family's value. The process is called SWEEP, but don't worry—I'm not asking you to start cleaning the floors. It's an acronym for a process that can act as a litmus test for how you're doing in life. When there's a lot going on, this method is a way of focusing on the bare bones of what you need to be in a good place. If you're struggling or can't pinpoint what exactly is creating the friction in your life or those of your children, the best starting point is to look at the components of SWEEP. Here's how it breaks down.

S—Sleep

Sleep matters more than you may realize. The approximately seven to nine hours of downtime that an adult's brain and body need to recharge must not only exist but also be of high quality. Without essential rest on an ongoing basis—both quality and quantity—you will become worn down and put yourself at risk of health problems including obesity, depression, memory loss, heart disease, and more. You simply cannot be the best version of yourself for you or your family if you're not prioritizing rest.

As I write this, we are still dealing with the Covid-19 pandemic in significant ways. The impact it has had on our sleep is just one of them, so keep this in mind as you assess how you're treating yourself. According to a recent study, 36 percent of people globally have experienced sleep problems during the pandemic due to stress, work schedule disruptions, health issues, and more. Similarly, according to the American Psychological Association, 32 percent of US adults reported that the pandemic had impacted their sleeping habits. Seems to me that now's an important time to look at your "S" in SWEEP and your zzzzzs.

So ask yourself: "Am I getting enough sleep? Do I feel rejuvenated when I wake up? Do I lie in bed for hours before my body finally rests? Do I have night terrors or sleepwalk? Is my own or my partner's snoring disrupting me? Do I scroll on social media until the middle of the night because I'm not prioritizing sleep? Do I treat getting into bed by a certain time as seriously as I heed my alarm clock in the morning?" Some of the changes you need to make will be in your own hands as you take sleep more seriously and set yourself up for success with proper sleep hygiene (yes, that's a thing). You might just need a magnesium supplement, or you could have more serious unaddressed health issues causing sleep disruption. Don't jump ahead of yourself, because at this point as you SWEEP, you don't yet need to pinpoint it or get support from a healthcare practitioner. You're simply accumulating important information so you know where you stand and what needs healing, not recognizing the underlying issues or implementing solutions just yet.

You need solid sleep for your own sake, but know that the example you are setting with your sleep habits also impacts your kids. If your own sleep is less than ideal, chances are high that the bedtime routine in your home lacks the structure that would fulfill the physical and emotional needs that you and your kids have. Your children need role models who value sleep to grow up with steady structures and rituals around this significant component of everyone's health and well-being. Depending on their specific age, kids older than three years typically need ten to fourteen hours of shut-eye a night. Insufficient sleep could be at the source of behavior issues and poor decision making. It's essential for children's development, so treat it as such.

W—Work

What I'm calling "work" here doesn't necessarily mean a nine-to-five office job. I'm talking about however many hours a day you spend utilizing physical and mental energy toward a targeted result. Do you have a purpose to your day? Are you achieving that purpose regularly? How do you feel about that purpose, meaning is it authentic to you and truly fulfilling or just a placeholder that sucks your time and leaves you feeling empty?

Covid-19 has had an unprecedented impact on our work life. From remote work blurring the boundaries we once had to the Great

Resignation that saw forty-seven million people quit their jobs, the "W" in our SWEEP has had far-reaching disruptions. Stay-at-home parents found their existence turned upside down when schools closed their physical doors and had kids resort to online learning, often requiring parents to fill the inevitable gaps. Some parents who worked from home may have had more quality time with their families in lieu of a commute; others have found themselves drowning in the stress of working and parenting concurrently in the same space. Often, parents experienced both. Whether your work life took a beating or you and your family have significantly benefited from a new normal, the outbreak is yet another reason to focus on this dimension of your life. We each need endeavors from which we derive a sense of accomplishment, just as we need time away from those efforts to recharge. They're two sides of a coin, and both are necessary for a full, healthy life.

Likewise, when you do a SWEEP with your children, look at their experience in school from academic and social perspectives. Those are equivalent to their work, and they occupy huge places in your kids' sense of purpose and self.

- Are they in the best educational environment for them?
- Is their confidence and knowledge developing through an age-appropriate curriculum?
- Where do they struggle or need more support?
- Do they have appropriate and meaningful social interactions with peers? Have you seen evidence that both their IQ (intelligence quotient) and EQ (emotional quotient) are growing from their time at "work"?
- Since the pandemic, have you noticed changes in their relationship to school or activities?

I'm not yet asking you to research options that might better serve your family or to implement solutions. At this stage, we're simply doing critical fact-finding about how your whole family's work life is faring, from your time at the office or running a home to your children's experience in school or working toward their own professional goals.

E—Eating

Are you using food to stay healthy and energized? Do the foods you eat provide you with nourishment, or do you mindlessly consume calories that are actually depleting you? Do you eat the appropriate amount of food, or do you eat until you're so stuffed that you feel uncomfortable and then beat yourself up afterward? It's like the saying "Garbage in, garbage out," meaning what you put into your body has ramifications. This is great news, because you're the one who controls what goes in, which we can change as soon as we understand your current eating habits.

By focusing on blood sugar, we can get specific about the impact food can have on you and its power to wreak havoc on your entire family. For example, it always astounds me how few people connect the dots between low blood sugar and emotional or behavioral chaos, both for us as adults and for our children. (This is not something that only affects diabetics.) So let me connect the dots for you. When your blood sugar gets too low, perhaps from skipping meals, cutting out carbs, excessive exercise, or drinking too much alcohol, we can become restless, anxious, jittery, have difficulty concentrating, get headaches, and more. On the flip side, high blood sugar, known as hyperglycemia, can cause damage to anyone if it goes unchecked. Now, I'm not saying that every time you're feeling cranky, all you need is a Granny Smith to help your levels and turn your mood around. But when you feel subpar, your blood levels are worthwhile places to explore.

The importance of nutrition, of course, also holds true for your children. Are you modeling for them how to eat, what to eat, and when to eat? Are you taking the imperative to feed them as the consequential responsibility it is? If you don't know when their last meal was or you offer fast food regularly because it's the path of least resistance, odds are that your family is lacking the consistent habits of healthy eating that are necessary to thrive.

I'm sure there are many reasons why your teenager is incredibly moody, unpredictable, or depressed, but poor nutrition doesn't need to be among them. I recently saw a child with behavioral and learn- ing issues who was suffering from celiac disease, an intolerance to gluten found in breads, crackers, and many flour-based products . . . and that had gone undiagnosed for eight years! Doctors treated him with medicine for ADHD and grasped at straws for other diagnoses, but not once did a healthcare practitioner realize that a gluten intol- erance was at play. Similarly, I had a patient who was so depressed she became suicidal. Only once we discovered just how nonfunc- tional her thyroid was, which was wreaking havoc on her body after every meal, were we then able to get her to a better place. So take a closer look at what you and your family are consuming and how you're doing it, because it could be playing a chaotic role both inter- nally and externally. A medical intervention is not always necessary or required to pinpoint possible biological issues connected to food, but it's important to know that they're available and can be an inval- uable resource for many families.

There are other aspects of our eating regimen that have an impact far greater than you may realize. Do you use mealtime as an opportunity to fuel not only your body but also your soul? Do your children use meals to consume a healthy dose of calories in a timely manner while also having an opportunity to relax and bond with loved ones? I can't stress enough how important it is that parents do the best they can to eat as a family a few times a week at the very least. It's a time when your family should be undistracted, adhere to rules such as no technology at the table, and make eye contact as you connect over that day's events, share feelings, solve problems, talk about the headlines, and more. Everyone should have an opportunity to interact and to feel respected and comfortable. When you sit down together regularly, the overall communication of your family is strengthened, as is the parent-child dynamic and the bonds among siblings. It's during mealtime that your child might open up about being bullied, an academic struggle, or peer issues that are weighing on them, and it's during mealtime that they can feel supported, heard, and seen. There are numerous studies proving the benefits of sitting down together for meals, including lower rates of depression, anxiety, and substance abuse, higher self-esteem, better academic performance, and increased resiliency.

It's a critical time to nourish bodies, brains, and souls—our own and our children's—so don't squander it.

E—Emotional Expression

For you to be emotionally healthy, you need to be in touch with your thoughts and feelings. Not only that, but you also need to be able to express them. So ask yourself: "Do I allow myself emotional intimacy? Do I value it? Do I let the important people in my life, especially my partner and kids, know how I'm feeling through emotional expression?" Each relationship needs to be nurtured regularly.

Think about an exasperated, emotional child who can't seem to convey what's getting them bent out of shape. Time and again you've probably heard an adult tell them, "Calm down, use your words so I can understand what's going on for you!" Just as a child can struggle to express complex or negative emotions, adults also can find it difficult to access their feelings and emote. If you're not able to communicate what you're thinking and how you're feeling, it will be incredibly difficult to connect with the people around you to establish the emotional safety and sense of permanence we all need.

As with all aspects of SWEEP, your child is watching you and learning from you. How are you role-modeling the way you communicate thoughts and feelings, if at all? Do they see feelings being articulated with authenticity, vulnerability, honesty, and respect when they watch their parents communicate and express feelings? How about when you're dealing with them? Do you use words to tell them how much you love them, or do you struggle to get the words out? If it's the latter, what prevents you from wearing your heart on your sleeve?

Our brains assign an emotion to every experience or thought we have. Ideally, to have balance between our thoughts and feelings, it should be a 50/50 split when we communicate: 50 percent of your thoughts and 50 percent of your feelings should equal 100 percent of your emotional expression. Said differently, our expressions should be 50 percent from the head and 50 percent from the heart, and combined they exit your mouth in 100 percent of your emotional expression.

To make it easier to remember, let me demonstrate with what I've drawn below.

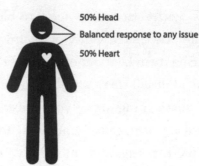

Our emotional expression is a huge factor in our overall health, and here is another area where Covid-19 created a troubling disruption in our development and emotional health. When we masked up, we also masked important emotions and relationships. Mask wearing has significantly altered the way we perceive emotion and nonverbal cues, which affected how we connect with one another. The change in the landscape of our social interactions ties to the numerous studies showing a decline in mental health. The social isolation experienced in the pandemic affected kids of all social classes, particularly girls. Kids also experienced an increase in social media use when their in-person lives came to a screeching halt. That, too, impacted their emotional expression, as we saw an uptick in online bullying, anxiety disorders, and kids experiencing feelings of sadness. It's important to consider whether this part of your life and your kids' lives needs a postpandemic reboot.

P—Play

Try to show me somebody who doesn't enjoy playing and I'll show you someone who's either hiding or hurting. We're all human, and whether we like to admit it or not, we like to have fun. Unfortunately, there are many reasons why we're either not permitting ourselves to have a good time, or we don't know how to. And as the old saying goes, "All work and no play makes Jack a dull boy." It can actually be far worse than dullness, so it's more accurate to say "All work and no play makes Jack unhealthy and can be harmful to him and his kids." Trust me, it's not a good outcome.

What do you do in your leisure time with the primary purpose of enjoyment? If you can't answer that question, the "P" in your SWEEP is lacking. It is important for all of us, at any age, to have activities that we can enjoy alone, and other activities that we can do with groups and friends. Ideally these activities would be in a range that keep you fit both physically and mentally, give you a creative outlet, and maybe even enable you to network or enhance other areas of your life. Most of all, whatever your version of play entails, it should bring you enjoyment and pleasure. Clearing out your inbox or organizing your closets do not count! I said "fun," not just productive or worthwhile. Partying doesn't count here, either; it's one thing to enjoy being social in a group, but the point of the play that I'm talking about here is fun that helps you connect with the most joyful parts of yourself.

Play is a critical ingredient to your overall functioning, so don't think of this as a frivolous endeavor or a bonus part of life. It is no exaggeration to say that it can be life-sustaining to find the right "P." The benefits of play include learning how to self-soothe, shifting out of a bad mood, managing anxiety, maintaining an individual identity, and broadening your perspectives. (And those are all in addition to just having a good time in the moment!)

Another reason it's important for parents to have an outlet for play is that it gives your children a model for reaping all those same benefits. They need to see parents who have fun and enjoy their lives. They also need to be encouraged to develop their own interests that bring them joy, excitement, and engagement. Hobbies, for example, help develop children's self-confidence as well as their ability to self-soothe when they have an interest or aptitude for something that makes them feel good. Play is an essential component for creating a healthy balance among all the letters in your SWEEP. So if you're not playing, it's time to understand what's holding you back.

Parenting begins with you, so only after you feel balanced and secure can you be the parent you're capable of being. You deserve a healthy and fulfilled life, and you need to have one to be a living template for your child. When you are in a healthy place, physically and mentally, you are a better parent to your child, a better role model, and a better you. SWEEP is an easy and informative way to teach your child about key aspects of life and to role-model these important components of well-being. Teaching them how to do a SWEEP on themselves gives you a baseline position from which to safely and appropriately open a dialogue about any of the components as you move forward and alerts you to any possible red flags that would likely have gone unnoticed without a SWEEP as soon as possible. When SWEEP becomes a regular part of your life, you also give your children the gift of knowing they can safely come to you about any information they gather from their SWEEP without being judged.

So get SWEEPing. Start with yourself, and then to gain a full understanding of how you're all doing, SWEEP your spouse, children, and family unit as a whole. In a perfect world, we'd like to have all five of these key life areas in pretty good shape. But we do not live in a perfect world, nor is our goal to help you be a perfect person. On top of that, we all have stresses and other issues that arise, so no matter how much we may think we're crushing our SWEEP, any one of these areas can unexpectedly go sideways and impact others along the way. But by having a reliable, simple mechanism in place to take inventory regularly, you'll be able to measure whether you're making progress and be equipped to tip the scales toward balance and well-being. My rule of thumb is that if you don't feel good about at least three of the letters, it's time to ring the alarm bell and buckle down. But when you do your SWEEP, don't just focus on your family's weaknesses or areas that need improvement, and don't single out any one family member to the point that they feel shame or failure. This is also an opportunity to look at your strengths. Pat yourself on the back for what you're doing right, and point out to your children where their SWEEP has positive aspects.

At this point, all you need do is take an in-depth look at these five dimensions of your life and record your findings. I want to reiterate that it is not all on your shoulders to remedy the issues you're beginning to uncover. In some cases you might need medical support to help you pinpoint and understand all the relevant data. For example, you might think that nine hours of sleep are right on target for your teen, when in fact thyroid issues are unknowingly sapping their strength. Inflammation could be to blame for the headaches that impair your work; undiagnosed depression could be the underlying reason why you have no desire to play. I created this tool because there are so many pieces to this puzzle, each of which has the capacity to disrupt your home life. SWEEP simplifies them, organizes them, and helps you see which pieces may be bent out of shape, as well as which ones are strong and well-positioned.

I believe wholeheartedly that these five aspects of our life are the "guts" of our health and at the core of our capacity to thrive as parents and beyond. In fact, I see them as so critical that I suggest that when you and your children have an annual physical, you partner with your physician to SWEEP. A thorough doctor should be asking these questions about you, your spouse, and your kids, but not all do. If your children's height is measured and you find out what percentile they are when compared to peers but your physician doesn't inquire about their sleeping and eating habits, that's concerning to me. If your doctor says "Not to worry, they'll grow out of it" about a child eating only Cheetos and French fries, that is also concerning. Accept nothing at face value, and use SWEEP to help you set the priorities for your attention. If anybody on your care team doesn't agree with their importance, it's time to reevaluate that teammate.

There's no official tally for how you're doing at life, but SWEEP is a straightforward tool that simplifies the most essential aspects of your functioning. If you're stuck, confused, or unsure where to start the work of turning things around, begin with these five elements. For so many reasons, kids need parents who have done their SWEEP. At the top of the list is that you're their role model for these critical components of life, and because they need a parent who has done a SWEEP and has the strength of mind and body to run a family. A stable parent = a stable child = a stable family.

Creating Your Road Map

The purpose of the SWEEP is to get you the information you need to make a plan to restore health and happiness. The hope is for each individual and the family unit to work together in taking this data to create a new road map filled with common goals, but we must also respect each person's authenticity within that process. Never lose sight of the fact that you are the most significant role model for your children, and the dynamics of your family at large also impact your children and their behavior. So when it seems you're not all working toward the same purpose, the behavior you model is a worthwhile starting point.

Take the information from your SWEEP and make a list for each of the five components—for yourself, for your children, and for your family as a unit. What behaviors do you notice each of you is exhibiting, and where does each of you need to focus? What are the common denominators that define the family's overall way of functioning? For example, let's start with sleep. Perhaps you can't get your kids out of bed in the morning, or you're bringing a crying little one into your bed in the middle of the night. In this case, getting your SWEEP in order requires a focus on sleep. This might mean that each member of the family needs to commit to being in bed by a set time. It could mean cutting out caffeine, sugar, or screens by a certain hour, coupled with getting everyone else in their own beds consistently. Have a conversation with all the parties involved in the new sleep plan, and explain in age-appropriate language why you're putting these new boundaries in place. As you design and implement a better sleep regimen for all, you are the starting point, but the entire family's journey gets mapped out.

Next you'll look at how you and your family fared in terms of work. If Mom can't stand her job, Dad travels nonstop, and the kids dread school, there's a lot of room for improvement. What are the next steps? Some ideas might include asking for a modified travel schedule, setting boundaries around meetings or reducing after-hours events to ensure a more consistent presence at home. In some instances it might be as extreme as a parent applying for a new job or going back to school to find a new career that's more closely aligned with what works for your family. When it comes to kids, addressing issues that come up could involve making an appointment to speak with teachers, administrators, or coaches, or requesting to have your children assessed.

As for eating, your road map might entail sitting down together as a family a minimum of three nights a week, cooking healthier food instead of ordering in, restricting devices at the table, or getting up early to pack nutritious school lunches. When it comes to emotional expression, you might uncover that parents need more opportunities to connect with one another and nurture their relationship, so a monthly date night becomes essential. Or perhaps your biggest stumbling block is teaching the children how to communicate better so they stop fighting. Likewise, with play it could be as simple as carving out time for the knitting that you love, or it could involve deeper work to uncover why it's so hard for you let down your guard and find pleasure.

SWEEP Road Map

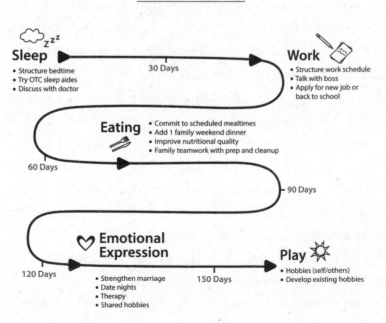

Do this process for each component of SWEEP, identifying areas that are most ripe for betterment, for your own sake and with the knowledge that your kids are learning from you. Then do it for each of your kids, your spouse, and your family as a whole. If restructuring and redesigning your family seem overwhelming at times, remember that this is how you are increasing your family's long-term value. Depending on the age of your children, you might share the road map you've all created so they can see it laid out and refer to it as needed. When you have set goals and action steps for each component that needs attention, you'll have created the most valuable road map you'll ever follow.

CHAPTER 7

The Five Essentials
of Your Family Portrait

Once everyone's inventory has been assessed and you're beginning to repack your bags, you'll be best equipped to do the work in this chapter about establishing a new way of looking at your family unit. If you think of SWEEP as a tool that disrupts the negative cycle your family has fallen into, this exercise will help you create a new sense of purpose and identity with stronger boundaries and expectations in place to keep everyone on track.

Think of your family values as a family portrait. Wherever you are in your life as a parent, this metaphor can help you grasp the different components of what it takes to keep that portrait a one-of-a-kind masterpiece. A flawed, imperfect one at times, of course, but a beautiful, strong, authentic, purposeful piece of art all the same. So let's understand each aspect of your most precious possession.

This painting is valuable and ought to be safeguarded with a glass cover and active care. These are your family's cultures and traditions, which further protect your family and keep everything in place. The portrait itself is your family's life. Like any good painting, yours is unique. To hold that picture together firmly, you need a frame, which is a strong identity as a unit, a foundation of values, and your loving arms. Even in that frame, you've got to be mindful of keeping it safe and intact through an active process of tending to and protecting it; the minute you neglect it, it will get dusty or break, and you won't be able to enjoy and cherish the picture inside.

If you were to put this portrait in the basement, no one would see it or care about it. Instead, you would want to hang this picture in a prominent place so there's a constant reminder of its central role and magnificence and so you can proudly show others this work of art, too. Finally, you would want it to be hung securely, which is akin to having the wherewithal and foresight to predict crises and the stability to weather them. Sometimes, even when hung securely, that picture might shift left or right, but when you don't expect everything to be perfect all the time and can anticipate some movement without the painting being knocked off the wall, you can rest assured that this prized belonging will remain in tip-top shape.

In this chapter, we are going to go through my Five Essentials of Your Family Portrait, which are the key ingredients to keeping that portrait's value. Quite simply, without them your portrait will become distorted or its essence will fall into question. So let's agree that family coming first is a nonnegotiable starting point, since that's what this portrait represents, and dive into each essential.

Your family's guiding principles are critical building blocks toward living with purpose, and they also helped construct your family's identity. Your family's identity is made up of each one of its members' self-identities and takes into account how your entire family operates at home and in the larger world as well. A strong family identity can help your unit live meaningful, joyful lives. It will be there to help you navigate through adversity, important yet tough decisions, and hurdles and barriers that every family can expect on having. Part of that identity includes your family's standards of conduct. It's important that every member of the family understands that there are rules governing behavior, because we are responsible for how we handle ourselves, how we relate to other family members, and how we behave in the world. Like a CEO would do to govern their business and keep employees in check, you must establish the code of conduct for your family. Build a framework of acceptable behaviors and rules that will serve to keep your family safe, respectful, and in line with your guiding principles. There should be room for individuality, so you must find a balance between a framework that is not so tight that it's unnecessarily constricting and not too loose that your family members don't have the boundaries they need.

One way to formulate these standards is to talk them through with your partner and the rest of your family. Having your children involved in the process will help them feel like the stakeholders that they are, give them insight into why the rules are necessary, and be crystal clear about what they are. This does not mean that kids make the rules—it's important that as a family manager, you hold firm on boundaries and make clear that the adults are in charge. But this is an opportunity to clearly articulate to every member of the family what those rules are, why they exist, and what they are meant to protect. When you present them as the frame around the family portrait, it is much easier for everyone to appreciate what the rules are designed to protect.

Get and Stay Engaged, or Showing Up for the Photo Shoot

A safe and nurturing family structure means that every family member feels appreciated and valued by everyone else in the family.

As a parent, it's your job to make sure that is the case. Too often, a child's sense of being rejected or disconnected from the family is at the heart of larger behavioral and emotional issues. To avoid this, you need to stay deeply engaged. Among running your household, working outside the home if you do, and all your other responsibilities, it can be easy to lose a meaningful connection with your kids—but you must not do so. Too often, members of a family lack a genuine relationship and function more like ships passing at sea— they occupy parallel space and get bumped around by one another's wake but never make contact.

Find an entry point for engaging with your child every day. This entry point needs to work for them on their time as well as working for you on your time. This looks different for every family and depends on how old your kids are, but this connective tissue might include family dinner, tucking each child in, helping with homework, or a nightly check-in that entails more than a distracted grunt from your teenager, to the point where you find or create a contained but consistent period of time to connect, when both of you can put down your devices and make eye contact.

Providing for your family financially is essential. I don't minimize how hard you work to keep a roof over their head and more. In fact, I think it's important for your children to know what it takes for you to get food on the table—just never in a moment of anger or to elicit guilt or gratitude. But what I'm saying is that paying rent or a mortgage is not a substitute for showing interest in what matters to your kids. Depending on their age, you can expose them to what it takes to support a family, and help them appreciate what you, they, and every member of the family can do to contribute to shared success. But as we discussed previously, a family needs not just physical safety but also emotional safety. Part of supporting your child is to give them your attention by marveling at their latest art project or by helping them navigate social dynamics in school. The minute you convey to them, in action or in words, "I'm exhausted from doing my job all day. Now what?" is the minute their self-esteem suffers as they internalize *You're uninterested in me, so I must not be worthy.*

Being present for your child does not have to take up an enormous amount of time; there are so many ways to grab opportunities to engage. It could literally be ten seconds of a special handshake that's your way of saying "I see you and I love you." Knowing your kids' schedules and engaging in their interests are ways to stay connected. When you're up to date about their school project, next recital, or just the latest hang-out with friends, you're better equipped to bond over what's top of the mind for them. If you show an interest in and support your children in whatever is on their plate, whether it's sports, managing a conflict, preparing for an exam, or anything else that matters to them, they will feel seen and trust you.

A great way to stay engaged with each other is to once a day, at the very least, find your child doing something right and say so out loud. When you see them hold a door open for the elderly person who walked into the donut store after you, acknowledge it. When they pack their own bag for the first time before a sleepover, say so. Whether you have a toddler who shares a toy or a college-age kid who competently navigates their newfound independence, if you make a conscientious effort to look for what they're doing well, you'll find it. Then take it a step further and genuinely share your praise. It need not be something tangible or a milestone moment; just noticing their good intentions can have an impact. Over time, as you focus on their strengths and growth, you'll be able to erase what I call their unsteady behavior. It's unsteady because it's still immature. These are vital tools that increase their feelings of safety and permanence, which, in turn, ensures that you will have a stable, connected family.

In addition to creating daily touchpoints when you engage with your kids, I suggest you create a routine that involves spending quality time as a family on an ongoing basis. I understand that always sticking to a set plan may not be feasible, but you've got to schedule quality time and then protect it. When it's prioritized for you and your kids know they can count on it, the positive rhythms of your family will become essential parts of the fabric that offers everyone security, predictability, and meaning. We're not talking about hours on end; it's called "quality time" because quality is more important than quantity. Consistency is key, so it can't happen just as a one-off. If there is something that stands in the way of spending time with your family, you must either remove it from your life or find a way to make it secondary. I'm not suggesting that you quit your job if that's what typically conflicts. But perhaps you need to skip some ancillary business activities, or sideline other commitments to spend more quality time with your kids.

You've got to treat time with your family as just as important as any other appointment you would keep instead of backburnering it or thinking that there's always next week for rescheduling. Would you cancel a meeting with your boss at the last minute to squeeze in a workout? Would you miss a shift because you needed groceries, or wanted to grab coffee with a friend? I should hope not unless there was a serious emergency. The same holds true for the time together that your family puts on the calendar. Showing your family that you show up for them regularly goes a long way. When family comes first, that's just what you do. And when you model that family is a priority, it will go a long way in protecting that precious family portrait of values.

Acceptance, or Letting Everyone in the Portrait Pose Their Way

In your family portrait, even if everyone had a matching outfit of khakis and a denim shirt, you'd want the individuality of each person to shine through. Perhaps their personalities would come alive with a certain pose, a smile, a raised eyebrow, a look in their eye, or any other nuance that exhibits individuality. Similarly, a safe and nurturing family structure leaves room for the unique traits and authenticity of every family member. What does it mean for your family members to be authentic? It means that each person has the freedom and support to be true to their own spirit and the characteristics that make them unique. Like those coordinated outfits, the family still has uniform rules and children are expected to follow them, even when they don't resonate. But also akin to those personality-driven poses and silly smiles in the portrait, your children need and should feel the prerogative to be themselves within their family's frame. Their individual essence is apparent in the picture, while they still operate as part of your family's whole. Fostering each family member's authenticity can become more difficult as your family gets bigger, but no matter how many kids you have and how diverse their interests, it's both imperative and feasible.

The goal of role modeling is not to create a mini version of you. If your kids feel too pressured to be just like you instead of their authentic self, if they are made to feel different, or if they feel judgment because they don't meet your expectations, the rejection will weigh on them, possibly for a lifetime. Are you encouraging your child to let their true colors shine through? Is it possible your child feels a need to hide who they truly are? Might they feel a stronger sense of community and acceptance from their friends, or even a gang?

I once had a case of a child with very nice parents who could not accept their daughter's sexuality. Ashamed of her identity and alienated by her family, the girl ended up a homeless drug addict. When the mother began to see the error of her ways, she felt terrible and found a way to stay in touch with her daughter—as long as nobody else knew about their connection. She sent her daughter very confusing messages along the lines of "I love you but not enough that I can let anyone else know." What the child needed was to know that her family's values included making her feel welcome, no matter her sexuality. She needed to know that she could count on them to provide her with physical safety and familial permanence while they worked through their disconnection. A child needs to feel like they are part of the whole even if they are different, as opposed to being ousted and alienated for who they are.

That may seem extreme, but the point holds true across the board that each child's individuality needs to be accepted and nurtured. Quite simply, if you don't allow your child to express their individuality within your frame, they won't want to be in your frame.

One way to practice the art of acceptance is by opening the door to different experiences. Incidentally, this can overlap with your new directive of spending quality time as a family and developing routines. Perhaps the first Sunday of every month you might explore a walking trail together or try a new type of cuisine. Show your kids that they are part of a family that can appreciate the world through different lenses, such as music, art, literature, science, politics, travel, sports, business, and so forth. The more exposure your child gets to those things, particularly when it's through you, the safer your child will feel discovering whatever most resonates or inspires them. As your child develops new facets of their personality and explores new interests, you are giving them permission to play in different ways. Not only does this allow for fun and create common ground but it's also setting them up with the resources they need to be resilient; a passion they find now may very well become the basis of coping skills later in life. For example, a child who discovers a love of art classes may find that drawing is a soothing mechanism when life gets hard. If you expose your child to piano and foster that interest, a connection with music can become life-sustaining.

By providing the avenues for your kids to become multidimensional human beings, their lives are enhanced, as is the connection with you, since you are the starting point. So once they show interest, it is incumbent upon you to help them develop their talents, recognize their intelligence or commitment, and support them to feel confident in what they're drawn to. You don't have to spend a ton of money on a new hobby or lessons every time a child shows a passing interest, but you can expose them to the full spectrum of what life has to offer and allow them to tell you when something sparks a passion.

It's not just about helping them set goals and work toward achievements, though that's important too. You should know, respect, and support your child's strengths and interests because those things are part of what makes your child who they are. Show up for their recitals, cheer them on when your heart is bursting with pride, and keep quiet when you feel the urge to criticize, particularly with teenagers. It's not easy, but if the goal is to nurture their interests and stay connected, which it is, then practice biting your tongue when that's called for.

As each family member embraces their diverse interests and shows their true colors, don't adopt any practice that is even close to joking or teasing them about it. Steer clear of any conversations that could exploit other family members. Even if you intend a comment to be said with love, or think that you are harmlessly teasing, self-expression in kids can get quashed easily if they suspect that they will not be accepted. A lot of families will pick some kind of feature about each other and rail on it constantly; it becomes the family joke both inside the home and in other places, where it could be more embarrassing. Don't get into that dynamic because it will eventually backfire. It could be used sometimes in anger or in jest; it's versatile. But in that same way, it can be versatile in the damage it can cause. Joking about little Johnny's obsession with comic books may seem like it's all in good fun, but little Johnny may develop a sense of embarrassment or shame, so much so that it could affect his emotional development and self-image.

Instead, focus on each other's strengths. Cultivate them, embrace them, and support each other. Use them as an advertisement for how great your family is. When you have each other's backs in this way, accepting and nurturing each other's authenticity, you certainly are.

Establish Your Family's Guiding Principles, or Constructing a Frame as a Family

What kind of frame do you want to hold your family's portrait together? The answer to this question requires you to clearly define your family's guiding principles. Like a business or any well-structured organization, you need a clear mission statement that articulates what your family stands for. What characteristics do you regard most highly? Could you put in order of priorities empathy, integrity, and hard work? Humor, worldliness, and financial success? Are there other central tenets to how you hope to move through the world, how you want yourself and your family members to be perceived, and what your legacy will be? The guiding principles are important for you to identify and for everyone in the family to clearly understand. How else can you expect your children to uphold your family's values now and for years to come if you never fully clarify and articulate what those values are in the first place?

Since you are the CEO here, call a meeting to order and discuss with the rest of the family what is most important to you as a person and what values you hope to be the underpinnings of your family. Your children, too, are stakeholders and you need their buy-in, so depending on the age of your kids, this should be a group effort. Aside from the critical conversation about what defines your family at its core, have each family member consider these questions:

- What do you love most about our family?
- What embarrasses you about our family?
- What about our family makes you most proud?
- What makes you want to come home at the end of the day?
- What do you want our family's legacy to be? What would you want to see your own children and grandchildren do and be?

These questions will spark conversation that can help fine-tune your family's guiding principles, and they will also reveal insights about where you stand as a family unit. You might learn where you are lacking in your parenting, where you are succeeding, and if there are any red flags you need to address.

Incorporate Cultural Practices and Customs, or Polishing the Glass Regularly

There's nothing better to deepen your family's legacy than strong roots, and roots come from history. Telling stories in your family about days gone by has so many valuable effects. The acai berry is known for being very small, but it can be quite powerful in aiding a healthy lifestyle. A family story is the same. It can be short and seemingly not momentous, yet have the power to give our children a sense of where they came from and who they are. This strong sense of family and identity is stabilizing, sometimes when it's least expected.

Imagine that after your daughter's high school graduation, she heads off to college on the opposite coast and moves into her college dorm room. She might feel lonely, overwhelmed, unsure of herself, or have any number of complicated emotions as she navigates a new environment at a formative time. But if you have done the work of building the picture, the frame, and the glass covering, then she is equipped to always find her way back "home," no matter where she is. She might, for example, seek out people, local places, or events where she can experience a feeling of your culture. When she has positive associations with her culture, she'll be more likely to seek out that connection, especially in a place with which she is unfamiliar.

Rituals, observances, or traditions can provide your family with added meaning and purpose, strengthen the fabric of your family, and offer safety and security during stressful times. If your family's cultural celebrations are integrated into your core values or are part of your everyday life, they will not only give extra color to your existence but also be readily available to comfort your family when needed most.

By instilling in your child a positive relationship to their culture, they will feel grounded, connected to their heritage, have an additional sense of meaning in their lives, and have yet another tool at their disposal for self-soothing, particularly in times of need. Said differently, kids without a strong sense of self and culture are more likely to turn to external forces to tell them who they are, and you may not like how that turns out. So make a conscientious effort to be the one who places that protective glass over your portrait with cultural ties and traditions.

For many families, attending a worship service is a key family event, or even participating in it so that the spiritual foundation is stronger. Whatever your beliefs are, the more you actively participate in celebrating them, the more your child will feel connected to something bigger than they are, a community and culture beyond the family walls. This could mean eating your favorite Lebanese food every Sunday, celebrating the Sabbath by lighting candles weekly, honoring your African-American ancestors' journeys to freedom, visiting museums that celebrate your Asian heritage, recalling your Mexican loved ones on Dia de los Muertos, marching in a Gay Pride parade, marking the Lunar New Year, fasting during Ramadan, visiting the elderly to honor those who came before you, or countless other variations of what your family holds sacred and wants to preserve. Identifying and prioritizing rituals is an essential way of modeling for your children what it means to make your family's guiding principles an active practice.

Whether you and your children connect with your culture inside your home or in another physical space, these are important ways to prevent that glass shield from cracking. And when you connect with like-minded people who share or honor your traditions, it's like getting prime placement in a respected gallery. You have an opportunity to show off your masterpiece and take your quite deserved pride in it.

Proactively and Progressively Handle Crises, or Hang Your Portrait Securely

The more securely you hang your picture, the harder it will be to knock it down. It still might get pushed sideways when someone bumps into it, but if you hung it well to begin with and have tools at the ready, you'll be able to seamlessly get it straightened out. Likewise, when crises hit, as they do in life, you're better equipped to weather them when you have a secure foundation and coping strategies. When you see any of your children not abiding by the family's guiding principles, it can be a warning sign that they may not be in a healthy place. We all lose our way sometimes. And when we do, it's easier to find our way back home when we know what true north is. Your family's guiding principles are precisely that. So when there's a divergence or disruption, there is no confusion about how to correct the course; the map, or the guiding principles, are always at the ready. Life is unpredictable, but if you know who you are and what you stand for, and who your family is and what your family stands for, you will get through the rocky times.

We've already covered what that secure foundation looks like, and in this chapter we've discussed your family's guiding principles as well as your culture and customs. Now let's get those critical tools in your parenting tool kit, because no matter who you are, life can serve you lemons. Or worse.

In the face of the inevitable hiccups of life, there are two key characteristics that parents should rely on. I call them the two Ps: proactivity and progressiveness. Most children, when they're the patients, will tell their parents anything they want to hear to break free from their worry and expectations. This results in the parents being totally misinformed about what's happening to their child, and, in turn, ill-equipped to make sound decisions.

Being proactive means thinking and planning ahead. A great way to help them develop this is to talk through their plans in advance, help them learn to anticipate what might be around the corner so they can be prepared to succeed. For instance, if they're going to a concert, talk through expectations of when they will be home and how they will behave when they're out. At what time does the concert end? How far away is it from the house? Who is driving, and is that person likely to remain sober through the concert? Being part of the process shows your kids you're open-minded; life happens, and you want to be part of the process for helping them succeed. The flip side of this—hoping for the best and then being upset when things go sideways—just sets your kids up for failure.

Having proactive conversations is a way to teach your child how to start adulting. Helping them think through and identify obstacles—for instance, thinking through how long it will take to get home so there are no frantic calls at curfew, having a backup plan in case the designated driver isn't safe to get behind the wheel—will allow you to have a thoughtful conversation about realistic expectations and ensure that your kid is in the best possible position to make smart decisions.

Being progressive means keeping an open mind when your kids surprise you. It's about letting them know that the boundaries and expectations you have for them are part of a dialogue and that you are willing to develop gradual, age-appropriate changes as part of the ongoing process of giving them what they need to thrive. That doesn't mean an automatic yes to getting a cell phone at age eight or three-hundred-dollar sneakers at age sixteen just because other kids have those things. But it does mean giving your kids a chance to make their case, and then working with them to establish how you might be able to find a way to work together to help them achieve the goals they have.

Being proactive and progressive can oftentimes feel like the most painful choice. But each time the two Ps are not the pillars of your decision making when you're in the throes of a problem, your family's portrait risks being knocked off the wall. When you lack the two Ps, you may be parenting on autopilot, which is essentially neglect that can send your child down a path that isn't buttressed by feelings of safety and permanence. That's not the path they should be on.

As part of your progressive approach, you will need to engage with your child's ability to participate in the process. You are always the parent and need to act like one, but your children can offer meaningful dialogue. When you collaborate with them, they feel empowered, invested, and respected for their input. You can still very much be the parent while empowering your kids to step up with their voice.

Admiring the Portrait

There is no more meaningful part to anyone's life than their family. While this work in this chapter of deliberately establishing and upholding the principles that define your family do require some deliberate effort up front, they will quickly become your go-to, reflexive approach to interacting with your kids and family. They can become second nature because they're in line with the way you want to be living. When you put in the work to keep your family portrait stable, your family will be living the values you most cherish. Your family will have lasting value, to all of you individually, to your unit as a whole, and for generations to come.

CHAPTER 8

Communicating and Connecting

firmly believe that the tools in the Sophy Method will help you steer your family back onto the right track. But a key part of ensuring that the tools work is establishing authentic communication and sincere buy-in—however begrudgingly—from every participant. As such, this chapter takes a closer look at how to have the deep, real communication that's an essential part of this process. Speaking as a parent myself, I know how common it is to hear kids say (or, more likely, shout) "You just don't listen to me!" And we all know that we've felt the same way in return. I want to make a point that's so incredibly important that I've reiterated it throughout this book: You're in a position of authority when it comes to your child. Even when it seems like they're ignoring you or actively defying you, they're always listening. So, to begin with, you need to take a deep breath and think about how you can tap into what your child is trying to tell you about themselves by speaking and listening in a new way.

Mastering the skill of listening to your child will save you from a lot of unnecessary conflict. Your child will tell you everything you need to know once you develop the ability to simply just listen to them. Listening means not interrupting them and letting them complete their sentences and thoughts. It means holding your advice, your comments, and your reactions until a point comes in the conversation where your child asks for your opinion; it also means knowing that that point might not come. It might even get to a place where you must have an agreed-upon code word or signal by which each of you will let the other know when you're done speaking. In this way they don't cut you off, and they can speak without interruption. It means no shaking of your head or sending any kind of nonverbal message to your child while they're talking because you're just taking it all in without judgment. It means not just hearing the words coming out of your child's mouth but also reading their facial expressions and body language. It means using all of your senses as you listen so you can understand the verbal and nonverbal messaging coming from your child and receive the full message that they're intending to send.

Actively listening means you absorb everything with under-standing and empathy before you have any response. When you are actively listening, you will not have to ask too many clarifying questions. This creates a setting in which the sender must be as straightforward as possible in sending their message. If the listener is not actively listening, I can almost guarantee you that the questions asked to clarify the sender's message will be of little value, which will frustrate the sender and often cause them to clam up. When the listener is quiet, the sender will fill in more details and will likely talk themselves to the heart of the issue. This cannot happen if you are not actively listening! Even if what you're hearing is upsetting or disappointing, making the choice to listen first with empathy will actually help regulate your own emotional reaction.

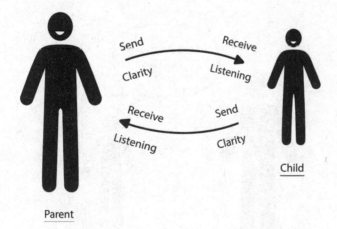

Remember that in every interaction, there's a sender and a re-ceiver. You and your child will play the role of sender and receiver at one time or another. The receiver couldn't receive if they only hear but don't listen to the sender, just as the sender couldn't send a mean-ingful message if they weren't listening and receiving before they became the sender. There are requirements for the communication circle to be influential, whether you're the sender or the receiver, the parent or the child. These requirements include active listening, self-control, and respect, as well as trusting that the other person is coming from a well-intentioned place and not trying to hurt you. With that as the foundation, listening to—not just hearing—the other person while they're speaking will allow you to receive their intended message so that you can formulate a response. Many times one or both parties are emotional or don't trust the other person's intentions, and are therefore unable to actively listen and may become disrespectful and/or lose control. You must maintain self-control and respect, which means no eye rolling or using other offensive body language. If you're purposely trying to trigger the other person while they're talking to you, then it's not a productive time to engage.

The ability to communicate openly and honestly with your child is of vital importance. The image of the parent with tape over their mouth signifies the value of actively listening and paying attention in a respectful way to your child as they're speaking and sending you a message that they will undoubtedly require feedback. Role-modeling the way you want them to behave when you speak again has to start with you. Doing that on a regular basis will provide the emotional safety your child needs to be vulnerable and express themselves honestly.

So how do you actually put this into practice, particularly if your child is doing or sharing something that's eliciting a big reaction? Think of it as 50 percent from your brain, and as it comes down from your brain, it will meet the other 50 percent from your heart to then produce a well-thought-out message. This is the best package to send a message to your child. When you do the hard work to make sure that you are approaching your child with a message that is clear, simple, and understandable, your child will in turn be able to receive the message from a place of calm.

Learning to Unhook and Look

Too often there is a disconnect between your internal and external messages. This can happen when disappointment is expressed without affirming love; it can happen when a reaction comes before active listening; it can come simply through body language. Having your child receive the wrong message due to the conflicts within yourself or your triggering body language will be a setback in your efforts to communicate successfully with each other. The aftermath and cleanup that often ensue may present you with a problem that is double or triple the magnitude of what you may have started with.

Now, I'm not saying that you, the parent, has to have every message clear, concise, and accurate before beginning a communication loop with a child. It's acceptable to have conflicting internal messages along with a level of emotionality that may be difficult to control at that moment. In those instances I tell parents to unhook and look. Understand and acknowledge that you may have an internal conflict that prevents you from sending your child a clear and concise message. By stepping back and unhooking from the situation, you can give yourself some perspective on it. By looking, you can allow your emotional temperature to drop. Once that has happened, your logical brain will be able to reengage and enter the situation from a position of control rather than discomfort, incongruency, or panic and allow you to package your message with little to no conflict, ensuring successful delivery.

I tell many parents in times of crisis, especially when communicating with their child, to take a deep breath, take a step back, and think hard about how to send your message so your child will benefit from it. Don't make the mistake of underestimating the power of positive self-talk. Positive self-talk is an internal dialogue mechanism that can motivate you to participate in a conversation from a place of strength and calm. It's the voice inside you that can help you look at the glass as half full in moments when it feels half empty. Examples of positive self-talk when communicating with a child might be:

- "I'm a great parent. Not a perfect one, but a capable, level-headed, fair, strong, and intelligent one. I will not be steam-rolled by a teenager."
- "I feel anxiety because my own parent was absent for these tough moments, not because I can't successfully tackle this bump with my child and have both of us come out stronger."
- "Even if this conversation doesn't end up going where I want it to go, it's going well so far."

- "I have the power and knowledge to control this dialogue; that's what I'm doing right now."
- "Even though my child is getting upset, I will remain calm and be successful in my communication."
- "I'm my child's best role model. I'm the parent and I'm in control."

By feeding yourself positivity, you can train yourself to eradicate the negativity that can hold you back. Positive self-talk can help ground you, and can squash the fear or insecurity that can sometimes derail your parenting goals. When you make positive self-talk a habit, you'll increase the likelihood that you'll say what you want to say and have it be heard appropriately.

The Messages We Send

It's essential for a parent to emotionally check themselves and quiet their internal dialogues and maintain self-awareness of their body language to get to the most neutral place before formulating and sending a message to their child.

You communicate many things to your child through your voice, your tone, your facial expressions, your body language, and your movements. If you roll your shoulders in a shrugging manner, it may send a dismissive message to your child even if the words coming out of your mouth are supportive. You could be conversing with your child, intending to have your child receive the message that you love them and care about them. You may be genuinely trying to work through an issue to come to a resolution, and sincerely want to handle the situation calmly and in alignment with your family values. But if you are also still fuming about how angry you are at what they did, how much they risked, and what the potential consequences of their actions might have been, you will still be in a defensive position. Your body language is more likely sending signals out of alignment with the compassion you know you ought to be extending to your child. You can be sure that if you have two different competing messages, the one that your child will receive will be as twisted as the two messages are within you. Therefore it's vital to ensure that you are very clear and solid within yourself before you send a message to your child.

The Power of Humor

Just like the adage "a spoonful of sugar helps the medicine go down," the same goes for your parenting. Your child will be better able to receive a message with a little bit of humor than if it's always with a stiff upper lip. Do you laugh at yourself? Do you make jokes about yourself? Do you try to send a message in a funny and joking way when it's appropriate? Does your idea of an authority figure include the ability to joke around, or is it all business? If you start to look and listen, you may notice that some of your child's favorite role models, especially teachers and coaches, deliver their message in a way that combines clarity and seriousness as well as a little bit of humor sprinkled in. Those are the role models toward whom children tend to gravitate. It is easier for a child to accept and receive messages even if they don't like the content when given with a smile, a joke, or some humor. This does not undermine the authority of that figure or role model—it makes them relatable and establishes an important dynamic of trust that is essential for good communication.

Humor is an excellent tool if used in the right way. I need to be clear about this because it's imperative to distinguish between laughing *with* your child versus laughing *at* your child. Be sure not to make your child the butt of a joke. Whether it's alone or around the company of others, the humiliation felt by your child can deeply penetrate their soul and have lasting effects.

Families who can find humor in their daily trials and tribulations or even in larger challenges are less likely to catastrophize any situation, and that same humor will help children avoid feeling a drawn-out aftermath of negativity. Humor can make an issue more palatable and reduce the likelihood that a problem will leave an adverse imprint on your family's psyche, and specifically on that of your children. I call this kind of humor healthy humor. And the healthier the humor a family has regarding a negative situation, the less traumatic the outcome. The aftermath is often less severe when healthy humor is part of the mix.

You may be saying, "Well, Dr. Sophy, we're laughing all the time in our family, so how do I know if there's enough humor? How do I know if it's that healthy humor you're talking about?" You'll be able to recognize healthy humor if it allows you and your family to be able to recall memories, traditions, and all kinds of crazy stories and times that you've shared over many years without someone being laughed at or feeling disrespected. The biggest distinction between healthy humor and unhealthy humor is how the story is told, and if a story is about someone in particular, how that person is feeling. If they're laughing along with the family and enjoying the memory, it's healthy. If someone feels like the butt of the joke, it's not.

Committing to the Process

One of the most straightforward and doable ways of engaging with your kids is by creating dinnertime rituals. I can't stress how important eating as a family at the dinner table without media is. It should be the simplest thing in the world, but nowadays it seems more and more difficult. How ironic. Put down your phone, make eye contact with your child, and have a conversation. This is a time to ask questions such as, "What was the best thing that happened to you today?" or "What's the most annoying thing that happened to you today?" and to talk about things that don't matter at all. This is also a time for you to role-model for your children your own comfort (or willingness to get more comfortable) with being vulnerable, connecting with them, and sharing about your day or whatever the topic at hand may be. There's got to be a give-and-take, so participate in a meaningful way. If your family is out of practice or in the throes of change this may feel uncomfortable or be met with some resistance. Don't be discouraged, and keep asking questions—eventually you'll find ones that will get them to engage. Consider a game called "Roses and Thorns" in which each person shares the best part of their day (a rose) and the prickliest part of their day (a thorn). For older children, you might talk about lessons learned from those thorns, or how those thorns could morph into roses. There are many variations on this conversation starter, so modify it to fit your family's preferences, such as adding something you're looking forward to (a bud), something they wish they could do over, or an act of kindness from that day. Just the facts that you're giving your child quality time, sitting down together over a meal, and creating the safety net they crave with a meaningful ritual are more important than you'll ever know. Actually, you will know, because you'll see the fruits of your labor in the present and for years to come. And the more you practice at the dinner table, the easier it will be to establish more points of connection. Because, of course, as important as a dinnertime ritual is, it shouldn't be the only place where your kids feel your presence and feel comfortable opening up. Take a walk and talk to your kids in nature, hang out in the family room with your feet kicked up, or find time to play or have some unexpected fun, such as a mini-golf or bowling outing. Let your children know that it is never a bad time to express themselves and you're there for it no matter what.

The more you have conversations with your child, big or small, the more you will be integrated into their world. With every moment of connection, the bond between you strengthens, which makes them feel more comfortable opening up to you when something weighs heavily on their mind or they really need support. Whatever the subject, if it's relationships, politics, religion, or sports, the more you talk, the more you teach your children to feel comfortable express-ing themselves. Their self-confidence will jump leaps and bounds when you provide them with a safe space for self-expression, as will your intimate connection.

Another way to get and stay engaged is by doing family projects. Might a family garden be up your alley? Building a tree house? Anything that encourages working together is a wonderful oppor-tunity for connection. Even setting the table, clearing it, loading the dishwasher, or taking out the trash as a family unit, with each person assigned a different task, is an opportunity for engaging with one another, making everyone feel like they have a place in the family, teaching the importance of responsibility, and modeling teamwork.

The day your children were born, you were given the opportu-nity to commit your life to them by raising them, building a family, treasuring them, and supporting them. Think of each day as an opportunity to re-up on that commitment. What a gift! Forgive yourself for when you've fallen short, and instead start steering your family in a better direction by engaging with your child. A safe and nurturing family structure requires you to be engaged and present. No one expects perfection, but every morning you've got a chance to do better, to invest more, to commit for the long haul to their well-being. Every day is a new start.

A Final Note About Employing Active Listening

Just as you may get some pushback as you start to shift the family's power dynamic back into a healthy position, it may take some time for your child to respond to your new approach of active listening. Give them time, and take opportunities to show them that you're committed to the process. Ask them questions in the car when you're taking a short ride so they feel like there's an easy exit. Follow up with them about small details to get both of you in the habit of sharing and listening. Engage them in decisions such as what to have for dinner or what show to watch—and then follow through with their suggestions so they know you're taking their feedback seriously. The more you can grab little opportunities to prove to your child that you are capable of actively listening, the more comfortable they will be coming to you when the big opportunities come up.

CHAPTER 9

The Most Important Role Model Your Kids Will Ever Have

We've spent a lot of this book talking about how adults can establish a strong foundation to become the consistent, clear, and in-control caregivers that kids need. But for as much influence as parents have over their children, it's important that children be prepared to navigate the world on their own. So how do you ensure that your child is living by your treasured family values when you're not around? As the most powerful role model in your child's life, everything you say, do, don't say, don't do, your attitude, your relationships, your achievements, your food choices, your exercise regimen, your work ethic, even the look on your face impacts your children. It's an incredible responsibility and a lot of pressure, but it's also an awesome opportunity, the best gift, and most impactful parenting tool you will ever have. Your child is not a carbon copy of you, but they are watching and learning from you nonstop, more than you can even imagine. Your example, your shared moments, your interactions, your silent moments, and more are all building blocks of your child's self-esteem—and the goal is to build not just a skyscraper but an entire skyline of self-esteem. And I must also tell you that it is never enough to tell your child what *not* to do when pointing out the behavior you would like to shift.

Many of us forget that children are concrete thinkers for the most part. And that simply means their thinking is much more black-and-white. For example, if you tell your child you want them to stop the behavior of yelling at their siblings, it would not be uncommon for your child to think they've been successful when they stop yelling at their siblings but now they start yelling at you. If you want them to stop yelling at their siblings, what needs to be said is to stop yelling at anyone or anything. Otherwise the desired behavior will never be extinguished and you'll find yourself very frustrated.

Knowing that, with every move you make or don't make, I'm essentially asking you to ask yourself, "Am I making choices and exhibiting behaviors that I want my child to emulate as they learn who they are, who they want to be, and how to move through the world? Have I mastered my own imprint and am I guiding my child from a strength-based, supportive place?"

I'm talking to you as a psychiatrist and as a parent. A significant way by which we communicate our family values is through our daily behaviors and priorities. The values we adhere to day in and day out become the values that define our family. No matter what age, children will always be impacted by the examples their parents set for them. You have the power to shift any family dynamic through the power of parental role modeling. You have the power to affect your child's trajectory with your own actions. Take that responsibility and power seriously; it's one of the most impactful tools in your arsenal and it's always at the ready.

Modeling the Behavior You Want to See

So many times I hear parents say, "I will not raise my child as my parents raised me." That's all well and good and is certainly attainable, but not without a solid self-inventory and self-awareness as well as a clear lens through which to parent. If that lens is not clear and if self-awareness is not present, you will run right into who you didn't want to become as a parent.

Your child is going to repeat and relive before your very eyes the many behaviors that you genuinely despise and have personally experienced in derailing your life toward places you would have preferred never to have gone. How many times have you said to yourself, "He's just like me, and it's annoying"? If you don't do have a clear guide for your journey through life, how will you able to provide the guidance your kids need to navigate their own? Whether we want them to or not, kids are inclined to copy our behaviors—the good ones, but also the ones we ourselves wish we could eradicate. Therefore it's imperative that we first have ourselves in check and know who we are, what we want, and what we stand for.

I can't even begin to tell you how many times parents have said to me in exasperation, "I just want my son to be organized and on time no matter where we go or what we're doing!" My response is, "Are *you* organized and on time no matter where you are going or what you are doing?" I already know their answer before they offer some version of, "Well, I honestly do my best with all that's on my plate."

What does that actually mean? It could mean, "No, I'm not," or it might mean, "I try, but I get overwhelmed by too many responsibilities and distractions," or perhaps, "Never in my life, and I spent much of my own childhood being told that I wouldn't amount to anything if I didn't figure out a way to get organized and on time."

So first ask yourself, "What makes it hard for me to be these things I want my kid to be? What do I need to be on time and to feel more organized? What can I do to prepare myself to get out the door without the stress of feeling disorganized and frantic?"

If you want your child to behave in a certain way or move through the world in a certain way, you must first master those skills yourself. You must live the example that you want them to follow, and then you must be willing to teach them how to find their own way of making those skills work for them. That's your role modeling at play.

Here's another common theme among parents who don't appreciate the power of what their kids see and hear day in and day out. "Dr. Sophy, I don't understand where on earth my kids could possibly get the idea that it's okay to talk to me the way they do," countless parents say to me with an earnest look of confusion on their face. "The level of disrespect and the tone of voice are unfathomable!" It's not long before we uncover that the parents are fighting in front of the kids, quite unkindly, and the kids are mimicking a toxic and inappropriate dynamic. The parent looks at me with an ashamed smile, muttering some kind of defense like, "But that's different!"

No, it's not.

Are you role modeling what you want your children to do and who you want them to be? How do your kids hear you talk to people, from other family members to service workers? When you're upset, do you calmly articulate your feelings or fly off the handle? When you're listening to your child—or anyone else, for that matter—are you staring at your phone or making eye contact? Are you communicating with ultimatums or with a back-and-forth conversation? Do they see you behave with consistency and equanimity? With kindness?

Think of this work as on-the-job training. By that I mean you're on the job, and you need to become your own role model and train yourself so you can train your children so they can train their children and so on.

Actions Speak Louder Than Words

There are two pieces to role modeling that are important for you to understand. The first one is this: role modeling in a nonverbal way has a much higher rate of being integrated by your child than verbal role modeling. For example, let's say you and your child are checking out at the grocery store, and as you're heading toward the line with the fewest people someone jumps in front of you. Your reaction to being cut off is going to make an impression on your child, all the more so if you model your behavior without narration. Many times I see parents go out of their way to manufacture a teaching moment, saying, "Watch how Mommy handles this with kindness," and they go out of their way to make room for the other. Or after it's over, they might say, "Did you see what I did that was nice even though I didn't like someone cutting?" Having to explain it to your child or telling them what you think they should be doing has a much lower chance of your child mirroring that behavior as opposed to saying nothing and nonverbally doing what needs to be done. Behavior speaks louder than words when looking for the successful outcome we want to achieve from positive parental role modeling.

Second, understand that you do not have to be 100 percent perfect 100 percent of the time. There is no such thing as perfect parents. There is no such thing as perfect children. Because role modeling is a 24/7 job, be kind and loving to yourself because you will no doubt exhibit behaviors that you don't want your children to model. That's okay.

I like to refer to what you should be trying to do as grabbing the opportunity. By that I mean you can and should be mindful of finding opportunities to role model as organically and lovingly as possible. When you can, plan ahead so you leave the house on time in an organized fashion when your kids are watching. When you're speaking with someone, look for opportunities to ask questions and really listen to the answers so you model for your child what that looks like. Grab the opportunity to model for them showing gratitude and appreciation to another. Grab the opportunities to model the behaviors you want them to learn—not in a show-offy way, not in an overly deliberate way but subtly, without calling attention to what you're doing. When you grab opportunities to illustrate the examples you want them to emulate, the chances are much higher that your child will model that behavior themselves. The pressure is always on as far as role modeling, but this is an easy way to make sure your children are seeing what you want them to see. Each time you grab an opportunity in these organic ways, the behavior your child witnesses goes inside them deeper and stays longer than if you bored them to tears with a monologue or rammed a didactic message down their throat. With every moment they see you doing the right thing, it becomes part of who they are as they develop respect for you and follow your powerful example.

Too many parents and families are heavily burdened by needing to work to support the family financially while simultaneously needing to care for their families. I understand how many directions you are being pulled in, and how desperately you need your kids to understand how hard you're working to meet their needs and just cut you some slack. How can you think about role modeling when you're just trying to make it through the day? But no matter how heavy or burdensome it may feel, I am here to tell you that you can do this. You can find the patience and the bandwidth to align your life with the values that you want so desperately to instill in your kids, and then role model those values one day at a time. When you can break the cycle of your own patterns that don't serve you well, when you can find your own method to be on time, to get organized, to listen without interrupting, to treat people with kindness, to exhibit patience when it's challenging, or any of the other big issues that you see your kids struggling with, you will set an example for your kids that benefits all of you.

Experience with our first family units created a foundation for how we behave in a family down the line. We will always be reacting to the behaviors that we had modeled for us (or didn't have modeled for us), and our kids are the same. But right now, you have an opportunity to reset the model. When you conscientiously work to model the habits, the mannerisms, and the behaviors that represent the family you want, you can break the cycle of whatever has happened in the past. That is why active role modeling is such a powerful tool for teaching our kids how to move through the world.

I always tell parents that behavior speaks, words do not. Know that everything you do behaviorally—not who you *say* you are—sends a message to your child. Ever heard of the saying "He can talk the talk, but does he walk the walk?" You should ask that question of yourself and make sure you are always "walking the walk"—when your kids are watching and when they're not. You are their biggest role models and they are emulating you even when you're out of sight.

Nobody's perfect, and it's as important to create a healthy environment to acknowledge our missteps as it is important to set clear expectations in the first place. When you don't live up to the standards of conduct that you and your family have set, first acknowledge this in yourself. That doesn't mean you should get down on yourself, but taking ownership is a powerful way to show your family that you are trying too. If you think your child didn't notice your lapse in judgment or your flawed behavior, trust me, they did. Fairness is a big deal to kids, and they will respond negatively if they suspect that you're trying to hold them to standards that you don't keep for yourself. So once you've acknowledged to yourself that you may not have heeded a code of conduct, let your children know. Don't make excuses; show them that you own it. Model for them that honesty, and then show them how you can recover in a calm, respectful manner. Exhibit the resolve you all need to see that following the rules matters. Your family's guiding principles depend upon it.

CHAPTER 10

Raising Confident, Capable Kids

magine jumping in a car to go on a long road trip without any direction or idea of how to get where you're heading. Where would you even end up? How far could you get without a plan? With parenting as well, we need to plan out the direction in which you want to go and the route you will take to get there, so that we understand how we each define success and so that our children feel safe and purposeful along the way.

Just so we're clear on this analogy, the road trip is your life, and you are the driver. And your job as a parent is to teach your children to drive, so that when it's time, you can turn the wheel over to them. Being a parent means preparing them to drive their own car down their road of life. Your children will only drive as well as you have taught them. They may not choose the same road you chose, or even that you had envisioned for them, but they will use every navigation tool you have given them to make their way down the roads on which they find themselves. So it is your responsibility as their parent to support them and give them as many tools as you can to find the best roads for their journey. What does that actually mean, in practical terms? Your job is to help discover your child's strengths and create a healthy environment that cultivates them.

Time and time again, I've seen kids living a life that feels like it isn't theirs. They're in the car but they aren't driving, even when it's their turn to take the wheel. Why? A lot of these kids have had parents who doted on them, did everything for them, worked hard to make sure that their kids had every opportunity handed to them. And therein lies the issue: These kids who don't feel control over their own lives have never had the role modeling, the guidance, or the independence to build the self-confidence they need to want to or know how to drive their own car. If you've spent your entire life with somebody else in the driver's seat, you've never had the opportunity to build trust in your ability to take the wheel. When you don't have self-direction, how can you master a sense of competency, self-esteem, or ownership? No wonder so many young adults suffer from a "failure to launch," lacking passion, self-sufficiency, and the capability to take on adult responsibilities. The odds are stacked against their becoming confident drivers if they never got their learner's permit! Even if a parent is motivated from a good place, they end up sending a message to their kids that says "I don't think you're capable." Over time, a child starts to believe this to be true. Alternatively, when a child feels that their life is built on their strengths, with their safety and permanence not in question, they're set up to uncover their purpose and their self-confidence thrives.

Understanding Labels

The labels we put on a child will stick to them like glue no matter how they come about. Putting a label on your child because you're angry is one of the worst things you can do. And once a child hears a tag placed on them by you, the most critical person in their life, they tend to step up and behave like the label.

I'm not just talking about overtly negative parent-child inter-actions. I am also referring to everyday messaging as well. For ex-ample, how often have you heard a parent introduce their child as "This is Mary, my social butterfly" or "Meet Johnny, my swimmer" or "This is Chris, our bookworm"? Although a parent may have all the right intentions in introducing their child in these ways, they're placing that child in a box with a label and not allowing them to grow in ways they have yet to explore.

I have a patient who's spent all her life not *really* knowing or believing that she's intelligent. Never mind that she got straight As throughout high school, graduated at the top of her class, went to an Ivy League university, topped it off with a prestigious graduate degree, and has had an impressive career. She still wakes up every day unsure of herself because she's trying to fill the void left by her parents, who were too hands-off. They barely acknowledged her report cards or impressive milestones like getting promoted to the corner office early in her career. It's not that they didn't notice or feel proud, but they came to expect her to excel, which can be a criti-cal mistake. Although children need to develop their own internal positive self-talk and sense of accomplishment, it's natural for them to rely on their parents to help fuel their growth and confidence and to give them the ingredients for a successful launch into the world. My patient's parents never managed to connect with their daughter in a way that made her feel seen, appreciated, respected, and valued. She desperately needed that from the most important people in her life, her role models.

I'm not suggesting that you give rewards for good grades. You may think it's nice to treat your child when their report card is solid, but in reality, rewards can take the focus off the learning process. We've learned that merit-based rewards actually push your child to be more focused on and incentivized by the prize itself rather than the process of learning and gaining new knowledge or insights. As the SWEEP says, school must be a child's primary Work, and so they need to know that putting in their best effort and attention is both expected and appreciated. Instead of accentuating outcomes, create a home that values the process of learning and then acknowledges each child's contributions and growth. If you can accomplish that, you will create a curiosity in your child's mind and an open-minded, confident passion that will serve them for years to come.

If your child lets you down academically, be deliberate in how you respond. If you have a big emotional reaction, take a step back and examine it. Where is that feeling coming from? Is it connected to anything from your past, or is it fully a reaction to the child in front of you? In your family, are mistakes an opportunity for learning, or do you leave no room for error? I hope the former. Don't insist that your child be "perfect" or hold them to unrealistic standards based on who they are. The more you react in a calm, emotionally safe manner when your child falls short of your expectations, the more they'll feel like they're in a safe space. This is another area where taking a progressive and proactive response will serve you— allowing your child to speak honestly with you about their learning experiences will help you understand whether they're struggling or need different resources or circumstances in order to succeed.

If you sense that your child could have learning issues, don't shrug your shoulders or assume that struggling is a natural part of their learning process. When academic difficulties arise, it can be detrimental to a child's assessment of self. If a child has an undiagnosed learning disorder, for example, that can be a risk factor for issues such as anxiety and depression. If you have even the slightest sense that your child may be struggling academically, bring it to the attention of the teacher or the school administration. Follow their guidance initially, but if you feel that you need additional support, I would consider requesting psychoeducation testing. This is testing done by a psychologist, often one who works with your school, to uncover more about how your child's brain is working, what the best learning environment would be, and what other avenues might support them.

Helping Kids Earn Their Learner's Permit

There are ways you can help to develop your child's mind so their cognitive abilities give them a sense of pride, accomplishment, and set them up for long-term success. This isn't just about achieving for the sake of achieving; it's about your child's self-esteem and growth.

How are you motivating your child to learn? How, if at all, are you modeling a love of learning? I'm not talking about lining your kids up with tutors or handing them flashcards at the dinner table. Helping your kids learn is about encouraging them to uncover what interests them, empowering them to take the lead so they feel a sense of control, inspiring them to be a self-starter, and creating a home where ideas are valued and shared. When you focus on whatever interests your child, you put them in the best possible position to become hooked. If your child has shown a love of chess, what's stopping you from researching local chess tournaments, or taking out playbooks from the library? Depending on your child's age, how about matching up with an elderly chess player who might be lonely? If it's writing that sets your child's heart on fire, there are countless online writing programs you can explore, or how about just handing your child a special notebook and a pen with a note encouraging them to see what pours out of them? Think about what a gift it is to give your children the opportunity to experience the elation that comes from loving learning and possibly a sense of mastery too.

To create a mentally stimulating environment for your children, follow your child's lead as they uncover what turns them on, and lead by example. Show them your enthusiasm for learning, ideally on a regular basis, and help them understand why it has served you well. Do your children see you reading, playing sports, drawing, or practicing other leisure activities? How often are you on your phone while you're under the same roof as your kid and everybody is awake? Do they see you express interest in world events, or do they mostly witness your addiction to reality TV? Do you know what they're working on in school? Do you discuss ideas, big and small?

One way to exhibit to your children that you're in it together is to ask questions. For example, if you're reading a book with your child about birds flying south for the winter, stimulate their thinking by asking why before the book reveals the answer. I'm giving a simple example here, obviously, but the idea is that you have an opportunity to engage, even if it's a topic that you know nothing about. It's more about the stimulation of your child's mind, especially in the early years, than it is about them knowing about the ins and outs of migration. Remember, the goal is to get their wheels turning, not to ensure that they'll be on the next episode of *Jeopardy!*. Be a champion; all you need to do in these moments is have a conversation.

Another way to make sure your children are stimulated through the questions you ask them is to be specific in your questioning. Parents will sometimes ask their children on the drive home "How was your day?" and of course their child's answer is "Good." Instead, ask about the gerbil in their classroom, what subject they're studying in a class, or a trip or an afterschool activity on the horizon. Not only will your child respond with more enthusiasm to the questions but you'll also feel more involved in their life, and you'll be more informed about what's really going on with your child.

Give positive encouragement to enhance their self-esteem and self-worth in terms of their ability to think, learn, and work hard. By encouraging their academic or intellectual strengths, they will feel a sense of competency that will position them to cope better when they struggle in other areas of their life. They will have a reserve of positivity to call upon and the resilience they need when they have inevitable weaknesses elsewhere.

Build your child a foundation made of their strengths. A strength-based foundation is the only genuine guarantee for your child to have the best possible future. Why would you rob your child of that chance?

Consistency

The world is variable and not always within our control. But when it comes to how you as a parent relate to your child, consistency is vital. Not inflexibility or unyielding rigidity but the kind of consistency that makes the rules clear, keeps poor habits at bay, and sets you up to maintain an individual and collective commitment to the values that you as a family expect one another to adhere to. When it comes to identifying and nurturing your child's passions or strengths, the same holds true. You must always send the same message in the same way to your child. It's a lot of work, I know. But if you help your children discover what they truly love, and then don't continuously provide them with opportunities to nurture that interest, not only will it be a lost opportunity to improve their self-esteem and competencies but you're also sending a message that you don't care enough to let your child explore and commit to the passions they want to build.

I have a patient in her mid-forties who still harbors resentment that her parents didn't find a way to make it financially and logistically feasible for her to pursue her love of dance on a more regular basis, an avenue that had the capacity to meaningfully contribute to her self-confidence. So believe me, consistency matters in the context of creating ongoing opportunities for children to explore and expand their skill sets. To do this, I recommend you create a schedule for your child that centers around their strengths and set expectations about how many hours each week a certain skill gets practiced or certain a hobby gets attention. This will not only set them up to feel good about themselves as they develop interests but the structure and sense of predictability will also lower their anxiety. There's a reason people relied on hobbies during the pandemic to hang on to their sense of self in trying times—because doing what we love feels good and is a way to self-soothe. As children get older, it's essential to give them more autonomy over their schedule, so they feel a sense of ownership and growth. Remember, you're cultivating their strengths and independence as they become confident and capable adults.

Building Resilience

As you partner with your children to help them uncover their strengths, there will inevitably be let-downs along the way—a poor grade, a crushing defeat on the court, a college rejection; the list goes on. This is where vulnerability becomes essential. The ability to express vulnerability in a healthy and productive way is borne from safety and permanence. People insulate themselves from the world to prevent themselves from feeling vulnerable. If they don't feel safe, how could they feel vulnerable? Your child will fall over and over again, especially if they're chasing something worth chasing. I can personally guarantee that life is going to knock them down at one point or another, because that's how growing up works. Nobody's life is free from adversity—and that's okay. You can't protect your children from hardship, nor is it your job to keep them from ever feeling pain, disappointment, or struggle. But you can teach them that they don't need to be afraid of setbacks and give them the safety and permanence that will contribute to their resilience in tough times. The more your child practices handling tough moments before they launch into the world as an adult, the better off they will be when adversity inevitably comes. Children who are shielded and protected from hardship or disappointments while at home rather than building the skills to grow from setbacks are more likely to then have tremendous difficulty navigating barriers they encounter outside the home.

This is especially true in the midst of a global pandemic that has upended our lives and challenged kids in countless ways. Whether it's adjusting to the challenges that Covid-19 presented or other obstacles that lie ahead, a parent's job is to set their children up to be able to respond with strength and resilience. By encouraging your child to try even if it means they struggle, by allowing them to fail on their path to learning to succeed, you teach your children that they cannot just survive setbacks but also learn from them. You can create a foundation so strong and impenetrable that your child feels invincible when facing the hurdles of life—not because they'll never fall but because they have the confidence to pick themselves back up and keep going.

PART III

New Starts and New Tests

CHAPTER 11

Negotiation and Motivation

t's a huge accomplishment to sit down and work on these steps with your family. But how do you get people to actually commit to the change? How can you take back your rightful place in the power dynamic while also showing your kids that their opinions and needs are going to be respected? This is when it becomes important to be able to negotiate with and motivate the members of your family as you begin to settle into your new normal.

I know I asked you to put yourself in your child's shoes and create a safe environment for communication and exploration, but let's not get too carried away. It is equally important to set clear boundaries. Good parents are not afraid to make a decision that isn't popular with their child if it's for the best of the child and the family. Think about that. Do you have the guts to do that? Because a lot of parents struggle with this, especially when it's something important or emotions are already running high.

Yes, you must allow your child space to make their own choices and decisions—even their own mistakes. That is how they will learn. However, you're also there to give those choices and decisions a direction—and, when necessary, parameters. You're there to give your child the information needed to make the best decision possible. You're there to tell your child that a glass of milk has nutrients that are good for their health; then, when your child decides to have a glass and likes the taste, you're in great shape. But you're also there to let them know after their third glass that drinking too much milk will make them throw up. It's your duty to teach your children values and discipline so they may lead a successful and healthy life—as part of your family and as an individual out in the world, too.

Negotiations at Home

Meet Brian, a seventeen-year-old with his much-anticipated driver's license. When he approached his dad to ask about helping him buy a car, his father listened and said he would discuss it with Brian's other dad. When his parents met privately, they decided, for several reasons, that they were not yet comfortable getting a car for Brian. They agreed they would set up a time to talk to him about it together. In preparation, they talked through what language they might want to use depending on how the discussion went, and used a whiteboard to write down phrases they wanted to have at the ready. They discussed who would open the dialogue, who would take the lead at the first sign of conflict escalation, and who would discuss specifics when it came to a timeline about the future, expectations, or the like. Some of the dialogue written on the whiteboard included:

- "Brian, I get what you're saying about having your own car."
- "Can you share with us why this is so important to you at this time?"
- "I definitely understand how you feel about it."

- "I wish we were able to say yes to a car for you, but we just can't at this time."
- "We both understand that you're angry about our decision, and we don't like to see you upset, but we're both hoping you can understand our perspective."
- "The way you're talking to us right now isn't okay, so let's take a break and cool down and come back to this a little later."

Brian's initial reaction was one of anger, and they did indeed all need to take a break to cool down. After the agreed-upon thirty-minute break, both parents and Brian met again. Despite Brian's emotional outburst, his fathers held the line with language such as:

- "We've given you our answer, but we're 100 percent open to talking through your feelings and hearing more about your thinking. We promise to take it all into account down the road. We may very well be more comfortable accommodating your request in the future, so tell us more about what's going on for you."
- "To be clear, we know how important this is to you. We don't agree with you that it has to be right this moment."
- "As parents of a brand-new licensed driver, we aren't comfortable providing you with your own vehicle at this time. We understand that you may not like our decision and that you're going to have a lot of feelings about it, but we would like to be able to have a respectful dialogue so that in the future when we discuss this again, we can restart this conversation from a solid place of understanding and respect."

- "We think it would be a good use of our time now to discuss what our expectations for you would be as you work toward earning your own car. We're open to it in the future, but these expectations are nonnegotiable."

In every family's history, some negotiations have happened that have defined how you and your partner interact and how you each interact with your children. Where does the power lie? Who calls the shots? Even though you may not think of your relationship with your kids as a negotiation, it is, and you're doing it constantly. Every time you try to reconcile differences, manage conflict, come up with a solution, ask for your child's thoughts, or discipline your child, you negotiate a change in your relationship. And guess who taught you how to deal with the family? Ding ding! Your parents! One of your first negotiation lessons was the first time you cried like a baby because you wanted to be picked up and you saw how your parents reacted. You may not have understood it, but you were learning how to get your needs met. As you got older, you realized (hopefully) that it isn't just your way or the highway. Or maybe you didn't—and if that's the case, I'm willing to bet that your relationship with your child isn't where it could and should be. Let's break it down.

First of all, I want you to understand that it's okay for your child to know that negotiation has a place in your dynamic. We negotiate in almost every interaction we have, and if your child understands healthy ways to communicate and negotiate, it will serve them well in life. The older your child gets and the better they can deal with things calmly and thoughtfully, the better your relationship will be. You'll understand each other's points of view, and when you nurture mutual respect, it will most likely lead to a solid relationship with your child for life. Knowing those characteristics will also provide insight into your child's various kinds of negotiations. Utilize each depending on the situation.

Often when people think of the word "negotiation," they believe that it has to be confrontational, like haggling down the price of a used car at a dealership. Get out of that mode of thinking. There are probably times when you negotiate where it is entirely non-confrontational every day. Whenever you are working with another person to find an agreed-upon solution, you're dealing. Choosing a movie to watch with a friend is an example of negotiating. Sure, that negotiation usually starts with "I'm good with whatever," but let's be honest, you almost always have some preference. In this scenario, you'll likely know that you like romantic comedy, but not so much that you say, "I want to watch a romantic comedy, that's what I like, and if you don't, too bad." You're likely interested in understanding what genre of movies your friend wants to watch, and then willing to talk about the specific options until you arrive at a compromise that works for both of you. We want to model and teach these kinds of negotiations to our children, whether it's as low-stakes as where to go to dinner or something bigger, like negotiating their salary down the road. You may have experienced a relationship with someone who refused to ever compromise or negotiate when it came to what to watch, and I'll bet things got to a point where it wasn't enjoya-ble to watch anything with that person. So think about this: if you can have a calm and open-minded conversation when it comes to a movie, you have the tools you need to bring that give-and-take negotiation when it comes to your child. Give every negotiation within your family the respect it deserves. Just like the movie situ-ation, it is possible for you both to leave the negotiation feeling like your most important points will be honored, or at least were thoroughly appreciated. That way it will be easier to understand where they're coming from and, more importantly, leave them with their self-respect and self-worth intact at the end of whatever negotiation is taking place.

I understand the hesitance you may feel about negotiating with your family. You've probably had failed attempts, times when you've butted heads, or maybe even times when one of the parties outright refuses to talk through whatever negotiation is on the table. Don't let your past attempts deter you; with everything you've learned in this book and your new outlook on being a parent, power dynamics, and communication, you'll be more than capable.

As your child matures, so should your relationship with them, which includes having more open dialogue and a more open mind in order to understand their perspective and really consider it. You, too, are growing, because you have a newfound self-awareness about not projecting your own issues onto your child, like forbidding your child from doing something they're perfectly capable of handling, even though that same experience may have been disastrous for you. Remember, your child isn't you, and you aren't your child. Listen to your child. If they're meeting your expectations, such as accountability with schoolwork and chores, there's no reason not to meet them halfway about something they want, even if you're not fully on board with it. Your only real job at that point is to make sure that they're safe and that those decisions are made with good judgment.

Now, even though this isn't a popularity contest, and you should never parent from a motivation to get your child to "like" you, you do need to see where they're coming from. Look at the root of the problem. I'll bet a lot of the issues that arise are in some way, shape, or form related to those pesky smart phones in your and their pockets. Trust me, I know it's tough, but it's part of your job to participate in the apps they use, ingest (some of) the content they ingest, and learn about the things they're exposed to. After all, you want to develop mutual respect. Only by doing so will you be more capable of relating to them and then approaching a negotiation with a better sense of their point of view. Too often, when I speak to the children of the families I work with, they tell me that they feel powerless if a negotiation ever comes up. Do you know why that is? It's because they feel like you don't understand them or what they're going through. The minute you can relate to them about things, and not by trying to use their terminology and slang (no one wants to see that), is the minute they will understand that you're in it together. Let your child know that you're there because you want to find a resolution. Let it be known that you want everyone involved to end up happy. A shared desire for a solution goes such a long way, and you don't want your child to feel as though your decisions are haphazard because here's a little secret: often, they think you're just shooting from the hip, and maybe you have been. If your child doesn't care about finding a resolution, it's going to be a tough go. But we will address that too.

Negotiation doesn't need to be a power struggle with your child. Every negotiation should have the same process, and every time you negotiate, you should use that. Remember the formula: 50 percent from the head with your thoughts and 50 percent from the heart with your feelings.

The Art of Negotiation with Your Kids

One of the biggest pitfalls I see parents run into is deciding what they think their child will want to be motivated by to shift behavior.

Just because you like something, or just because you feel your child should appreciate something, does not mean your child will like the same thing or be inspired to make a change with that in mind. You need to put thought, and I mean a lot of thought, into what speaks to your child—whether you like it or not. If that's what they will be motivated by, that is the carrot.

You may find yourself struggling to come up with that proverbial carrot, and it may be because you have overindulged your child. Maybe you have tried shifting behaviors in the past, and in desperation you flooded your child with anything you could think of that would make them motivated. Unfortunately, the move upsets the power dynamic you are working to restore—if a kid thinks that they can give you a little of what you want in exchange for a lot of what they want, they will be much harder to negotiate with. You need to reverse that and bring your child back down to the appropriate place of expectation. No, I'm not saying that your child will like that. You may get pushback. You may even have a battle on your hands. But you need to understand that that is the price you will initially have to pay for going to the extreme as you work to shift behaviors. Your child will ultimately accept the limits you're placing, but they won't do it without a fight. Can you blame them?

So the first part of the process is for you to clearly identify the target behavior—this is the behavior that you are looking to change. The next part of this process is for you to decide what currency you are willing to trade. What will genuinely motivate your child that you are willing to give without upsetting the balance? I'm talking about what makes your child motivated to do the things you need them to do, and that are good for them to do too. We all have a price, and you need to know your child's motivational hot spot. This is a time to be proactive, by having a discussion with your child about what will motivate them, and progressive, by allowing yourself to consider whether what your child wants is something that you're willing to give even if it's outside of what you'd been thinking. You don't have to say yes, but giving it honest consideration will make your kid feel heard and more likely to work with you. Make sure it's something that you're comfortable giving, and that it doesn't undermine all the work you're doing as a family. That will be the tool used as the proverbial carrot on the stick in the behavioral shift that you are looking to create.

The next step is to agree about currency and expected outcomes from your child. Everyone needs to be on the same page and come to a collaborative decision. This process of coming to this mutual agreement is the first step in role modeling with your child how the future bumps in the road will be expected to be handled by each one of you.

For example, Max wanted his five-year-old son to try to eat green beans. Well, he talked to his son, and his son agreed to try them if he could go to the park when dinner was finished. Max agreed. His son tried them and didn't like them. Max wouldn't allow his son to go to the park after dinner. When I asked him why, he said, "He didn't like them." Max confused a target behavior of wanting his son to eat his vegetables with wanting his son to be open to trying different foods. His son did *try* the beans, so in his view his behavior target was met. But in Max's mind, the target behavior was for his son to *eat* the beans. If his son didn't want to finish them after one bite . . . well, they hadn't effectively communicated about the expectations for the targeted behavior that was required for the currency to be exchanged.

I share the case of Max and his son to illustrate how this process will likely have some trial and error. Change isn't always easy, and every member of your family needs to be willing and motivated to figure out a way to make the system work for them. In some instances, there may be a misunderstanding—such as with Max and his son miscommunicating about the nature of the targeted behavior—trying the beans versus consuming the whole serving. And in other instances, it may take a little while for kids to accept that they have to commit to the behavior change to get the currency they're looking for. In these instances it can be helpful to have situationally appropriate consequences at the ready, too.

I'd like to introduce you to Adriene and her husband, José. They had a three-year-old daughter named Delilah. They came to me desperately seeking help to get their toddler to stop hitting others. They weren't sure how this behavior started, but for nearly six months, in response to anyone playing with her, holding her, picking her up, changing her, or feeding her, she slapped or pinched the person interacting with her. They'd come to my attention after someone witnessed Adriene slap Delilah's hand while Adriene was trying to check out at the grocery store and Delilah was trying to bite her mother. The anonymous call to the Child Abuse Hotline was backed up once we received the footage from the grocery store to see exactly what had happened. Sure enough, Delilah was attempting to bite her mom, and Mom did lose her patience and slap Delilah's hand.

Delilah's behavior had become troublesome on many levels, both inside their home and out. It was embarrassing to her parents, and at times it was painful physically and emotionally. We sat down to meet, and the first thing we discussed was making sure both parents were on the same page with a shared goal of shifting behavior. I told José that the first step was for them to take an inventory of themselves and make sure that the lens they were seeing their daughter through was as clear as possible so they could then come together to create a shared plan toward a target behavior. After discussions, self-inventories, and agreements were made about the currency, we were able to put together a plan to shift Delilah's targeted behavior of hitting and biting.

We then had an age-appropriate discussion with Delilah, explaining to her in simple terms the target behavior they wanted her to stop—hitting and biting—and the currency she would receive when she was able to control her behavior. The agreed currency would be watching her favorite TV show when she returned home from school each day. Importantly, we also gave her a series of other tools to use when she felt frustrated or overwhelmed—the emotions we identified as leading the target behavior that needed to change. The tools were things such as using her words, drawing her feelings out, or using her puppets to act out her feelings.

The next thing we needed was to establish how the currency would be doled out to Delilah. When you're in the initial phase of the targeted behavior shift, it's essential to have a continuous reward to ensure your child that you will follow through with your commitments the same way you expect them to. You lead by example and establish trust with your child that your word is good.

The currency schedule was that with four days of good school reports and no targeted behavior demonstrated in the classroom with her peers or at home with her parents, Delilah would then have four days of her television show. If the targeted behavior emerged when she was enjoying her television show, the TV was pulled back and the clock started over. This allowed her to understand that there would be consequences when she made a mistake and that she could earn back her currency when she handled her frustration using the tools she was given in place of the target behavior.

The exchange of behavior and consequence is vital for your child to learn at home to translate into their everyday world. Your child needs to understand that they automatically select the consequential path associated with that behavioral decision when choosing a specific behavioral pathway. Every action has a reaction, and the more predictable and consistent those are, the faster the child will learn. So when the currency and target behaviors were made very clear to Delilah, it was easier for her to learn that when she chose a behavior, she was also choosing an outcome. There was an even exchange process. And this was all done by the behaviors her parents chose as the currency that would motivate and regulate the behavior.

Because her parents were consistent and clear, Delilah was able to tolerate her frustration as well as her disappointment. She was also better able to use the tools she was given to effectively and safely express her frustrations. These are lifelong lessons given with coping skills that will allow her life to be much smoother than it would be without them.

Next Steps

Once a targeted behavior has become part of everyday life, you can pull back the frequency of the currency. This is an important part of the process. Suppose the currency is not pulled back to intermediate once the target behavior has been stabilized and becomes part of their everyday. In that case, it becomes very difficult for a child to move on to the following target behavior because they are satisfied with the continuous input of the currency they're already getting. Once the constant currency has gotten the targeted behavior to a consistent and stable occurrence, cutting back the currency to intermittent use will allow you to move on to the following target behavior. The next target behavior will most likely have a different currency. Again, it will be continuous until the behavior is consistent and stable, and then it becomes an intermittent currency.

The faster a targeted behavior is stabilized, and you can move to intermittent currency, the better it is for your child. Children who have learned quickly and maintain themselves on intermittent currency exchange are typically children who can be more flexible in life, learn to handle disappointment, and tackle the world without falling apart. Children who are maintained on constant currency are more fragile and unable to handle disappointment or anything that doesn't go their way. They are so used to getting what they want whenever they want it that when a situation doesn't allow their expectation to be met, they fall apart. This does not prepare your child well for life in general, especially for disappointment, a demanding teacher, an angry boss, or any challenging situation they need to work through. So give your children the most significant gift you can give them by identifying target behaviors and getting them stabilized quickly with a continuous currency schedule and shifting as soon as posted to an intermittent currency schedule.

When children have been taught with an intermittent currency schedule, they've also learned how to tolerate uncomfortable feelings, be told no, understand the beginnings of a work ethic, and delay gratification. If we look around at the world today, the majority of those having difficult times have not learned or mastered the insight to understand these feelings and the internal controls needed to manage them.

As parents trying to shift their child's behavior into a much more positive space, I urge each of you to be open and honest about it. Sit with your parenting partner or, if you're by yourself, sit with yourself and do the self-inventory that's needed and the lens clearance to target the behavior, and make the currency plan. Still, most of all, commit to seeing it through to the very end. Targeting behaviors that don't serve your child well and shifting them to appropriate behaviors significantly increases not only your child's self-worth and self-esteem but also your entire family's value. Your child deserves it, and your family needs it.

CHAPTER 12

Evolving Families

E ven if you and your spouse have a rock-solid partnership and an evolving family is the furthest thing from your mind, don't skip this chapter. Most of the strategies that I'll cover apply not only to families who are evolving or become blended but also to *all* families who want to minimize disruptions when challenges arise; keep communication lines open; coparent peacefully and effectively; and build (or rebuild) a stable, loving home. We'll cover principles that have relevance for weathering all different types of familial interruptions because, as I said, we now know all too well that our family's foundation should be as solid as possible so we own our fate no matter what the world has in store for us.

Over the past few years, more families than ever have faced massive disruptions in the family structure, including sudden death of loved ones, illness, job loss, home loss, lack of childcare, financial stressors, or the need to move for personal or work-related reasons. Couples with preexisting strains saw their relationship deteriorate even more, and the divorce rate increased by 21 percent. While I certainly hope we're not going to endure another pandemic anytime soon, the message is clear and remains relevant: our family unit must be prepared for crises in life. We as parents must develop the ability to navigate significant bumps in ways that provide stability, security, and success for our kids. That is what I am here to help with.

No one hopes or expects that their child will experience their parents' separation or divorce. But approximately 50 percent of marriages in the United States end in divorce—and that was before the added tensions that the pandemic has placed on our lives—so we need tools for navigating what I like to refer to as families that are "evolving." I prefer this word over "divorce" because it's an easier and more accurate way to express what happens to a family when parents split, and avoids the preconceptions associated with the word "divorce." Language choice can lessen both a parent's and a child's guilt and bad feelings, so we'll use that term from here.

When a family evolves, the kids' needs are heightened, so let's put all of you in the best possible position to thrive.

You Are Still the Parent

There are times when, after looking at the risks of staying together vs. the benefits of splitting, it becomes clear that an evolving family is the better thing for the parents as well as for the children. Nobody wants their children living in a war zone, which is often the case when parents don't get along. I always say that you'd rather your child be *from* a fractured home than *living in* one. But this is a very personal decision for any couple to make, and many people need to seek out professionals to help them get the perspective or strength to make the healthiest decision. When a family evolves, it has an undeniable impact on all of you. There are a few things that will likely occur, and it's important not to blow through them in your mission to help both yourself and your children. Remember that even if you had to cope with your own evolving family as a child, do not assume that your child will respond in the same way; each family and each child reacts and copes differently.

An evolving family presents new dynamics for kids to process and through which they must navigate to have their needs met. But those fundamental needs remain the same: permanence and safety. You are still the parent and they are still the child; that hasn't changed as the family structure evolved. Resist the urge to share raw, unprocessed emotions with your kids that put an undue burden on them. Don't make your child your emotional guardian. That's not their job—not now, not ever. The words "parent" and "friend" both have six letters, but that's the only commonality those words should have as you raise your children, particularly when a family evolves. The goal is to be your child's protector, provider, and leader, not their friend, even when you may feel the urge to build an alliance with your child or long to be the winner of a parenting popularity contest. That doesn't exist, but if it did, it would have an incredibly destructive tally.

There's a difference between being honest with your kids about your vulnerabilities and putting them in a position where they feel like they need to be responsible for your emotional health. Do not go on the defensive, badmouth your child's other parent, share your misgivings, or divulge your fears about money, loneliness, or any other aspect that is destabilizing for all of you. The parameters of your actions and reactions must reinforce that you are confident that your decision is the right thing for all of you. They need that reassurance. By acting in a calm, secure, and understanding way—even if you're crumbling inside—you are showing your child that the stability they desire is still there and will continue to be, despite the changes you're all living through.

No matter how you spin it, your child may view you and/or

your partner as being selfish for making a decision to change your family. To parent them with compassion during this time, you need give them permission to express their reactions, even when they're painful. Yes, you as a parent are also experiencing a significant disruption in your life. But whether you initiated the split or are on the receiving end of it (or anywhere in between), you have likely had some kind of agency in that change. As compared to your child, you've likely had at least a little time and a little more control over some of what has happened so far. A child of an evolving family, on the other hand, is being dealt an entirely new set of cards that are handed over without any input or power. It's utterly overwhelming, and it greatly affects their development as a human being.

This is when your kids need you—*all of you.* Your child may have just experienced what I call "emotional whiplash." People usually don't acknowledge this part of the process, but it's a necessary one: you need time for you and your children to mourn the loss of your family unit as you knew it. It's okay to be sad about the things that won't be the same, and your children should know that too. Not only is it okay but it's also an essential part of the process. If you don't allow yourself to feel the feelings of loss, you won't face those emotions head on and become stable enough to embark on this new part of your life—and neither will your children. Kids must mourn that their parents will no longer live under the same roof, that future family vacations won't all be together, that the way you celebrate holidays will change, and that the stability of their home feels different. If they don't find safe outlets where they can open up, their unresolved emotions will come out in their future behavior, which can be a recipe for disaster. So encourage them to talk through their feelings with you, and work hard to listen to them express themselves without hurrying to make them feel better or correct the record.

Your role is critical here, not only in terms of being available to them but also in terms of what you model. Now is a time to really dig deeply and reframe your evolving family's principles and values. Sit down with your kids and go through the family portrait exercises to remind and reinforce for them who you are as a family. Make clear the expectations for their behaviors in this new landscape. Do your best to create emotional safety for them, and remember to reinforce the boundaries of what is and is not acceptable regardless of those big emotions. The less dramatic or emotional your responses are, and the more understanding you are to your child's experience, the more solid they will feel and the more likely they will be able to move forward with strength and clarity.

A New Parenting Partnership

Now let's talk about the concept of custody. Custody is not a right; it is a privilege. All too often parents enter the custody part of their family's evolution angry, resentful, and disappointed in their spouse. They lose sight of the gift of being allowed to parent and what it really means to be a custodian for a child. Being a primary caregiver or sharing custody duties means taking responsibility of another person's mental and physical well-being. It means you are making a pledge to prioritize their safety and sense of permanence, sometimes at your own expense. So ask yourself if you *want* custody. Be honest. If parenting wasn't for you, or you discovered work that you need to do before you can be the type of parent whom you want around your kids, then now is the time to reevaluate what your evolved family model will look like. Amid your family's evolution, you get the opportunity to rebuild the relationship with your ex and also with your kids, creating a system that works better for everyone this time around. If hindsight is twenty-twenty, that's a benefit you've got now, so redesign the model based on what you've learned and what's best for your children.

Take any "rewards" out of this decision. The minute you see custody as something you can "win," you open the door to valuing things in the wrong ways. If "winning" is the goal, your child becomes equivalent to a soccer ball that will get kicked around. If who "gets" the kids becomes a sign of "victory," I can guarantee that child will wear the scars of parental immaturity for a lifetime. The amount of custody you're awarded is *not* a measure of the kind of parent you are, nor is it an indicator that you've "won." The only "winning" here is measured by your kids' well-being and your family's overall stability, so get the win/lose paradigm out of your head when it comes to your ex and custody.

If your ex is the one creating a sense of competition, it's incumbent upon you to defuse the situation by taking the high road. That might mean reminding your ex that no matter how much ill will there is between the two of you, your children's well-being needs to come first. It may even be worth copying and pasting this paragraph into a text message so that you get on the same page and understand just how high the stakes can be if you don't—without even having to hear one another's voice. In practice, this could mean biting your tongue when insults are hurled your way so that you mitigate the animosity rather than add fuel to the fire. Your attorney can also help you keep things calm by working with both of you to shift the focus from who, for example, wins the larger amount of communal property to who can play which pivotal role in helping your family as you all transition into a new way of being. When the rage or negativity is dialed down, each of you will be better positioned to negotiate as collaborators with a shared goal, not enemies at war with the kids in the line of fire on the parental battlefield. This isn't only about your needs, nor is it about vengeance or what's fair. It's about taking care of the human beings who need the best of both of you as they grow up. Your kids deserve nothing less than a custody arrangement that contributes to their safety and permanence amid changing circumstances.

Evolving Parenting

After a significant change in a family dynamic such as this, some parents will be parenting much more for the first time, because in the past they have shared or delegated many responsibilities to their spouse. Perhaps their ex undermined them, or they felt alienated, incompetent, fearful, or jilted. Perhaps the labor was simply divided differently. Some parents will be parenting less, which can be a blessing if the parent seizes the opportunity to develop themselves and, in turn, become a better parent. The more support you can give your coparent, the better it is for the kids. I know that's a tall order when emotions may be very raw or the relationship downright awful. But if you start from a place of being unsupportive, it goes nowhere but down for your whole family and can lead to a dangerous situation. Your kids pick up on all the verbal and nonverbal cues between you and your spouse. They hear the subtle insults, see the dirty looks, and witness the covert and overt sabotage. When kids feel like they have to take a side, it destroys families. Protect yours from going down that road by figuring out a constructive way to partner with your ex, no matter how hard that may be.

In some families where the exes are so unhappy with one another that they can't bear to speak on the phone, I recommend they use a shared calendar or a variety of apps that allow them to schedule events without needing to hear each other's voice or connect live. In some cases, a parenting intermediary with whom they meet weekly or monthly can minimize any triggers and be a positive step toward learning how to speak to one another on new terms.

When you have custody of your children, your job will be full on. Without another coparent in the home, you are the one in charge of navigating, orchestrating, and supervising all things parenting as well as running the other aspects of your household. It's an overwhelming new world. On top of that, you may be reentering the workforce, going back to school, or doing the job you've had all along, but now with less of a buffer. This massive juggling act can be daunting and debilitating. So put your ego aside and get real about how hard you're willing to work to have quality time with your child and ensure that neglect is off the table.

If in this new evolution of your family you won't be parenting your children as often as you're used to, you'll need to make sure that the time you spend with your children is well spent. It may be a cliché, but it's true: quality over quantity. Spending time with your children isn't a competition, and it's not about the number of hours. It's better to spend an hour of great time connecting with your child than spending a whole day with them being distracted.

If you haven't been involved with your children but are now committing to being an active participant in their life, you have your work cut out for you. Learn their routine from morning to night like the back of your hand. Learn when and where their dance or karate classes are and show up to watch. Get to know your child's friends as well as their friends' parents. It's called parenting because it is an active process. Kids thrive when they have a routine, so if you're sharing custody, it's important that your time together feels predictable and trustworthy. Don't throw the family values out the window even if you feel like celebrating every time your kids join you for your days; kids like presents and fun days, but what they crave and need more than anything else is your attention, your interest, and the sense of security that only you as their parent can provide. The best thing you can do for them is to use your time together to reinforce that you can meet their fundamental needs.

How to Parent While Moving On

My strong recommendation is that you spend at least six to twelve months single in the aftermath of a split. It's a time to take self-inventory, reflect on how your life is changing, and be available to your kids. I'll be the first to tell you that there is no such thing as a quick fix no matter how long you were married and no matter what circumstances led to your relationship changing. It takes time to deal with your own feelings of guilt, sadness, anger, fear, and countless other emotions, and to support your kids who may be experiencing similar feelings exponentially. Think of this time as a private family matter; there should be no one in the emotional space between you and your children as you get clarity on yourself, help the kids through the transition, and focus on the relationship between you and them. If you don't take the time to heal or you jump into a new relationship, you'll just be putting Band-Aids on the pain and discomfort, so instead of slapping on a distraction that might feel good temporarily, make the conscious choice to put your family first.

The dissolution of a marriage can leave your self-esteem low and your need for attention and companionship high. Finding someone to confide in and be close to can feel better than ever at a transitional time such as this. There are even studies showing that a rebound relationship may help your feelings of self-worth in the long run. According to a study from the *Journal of Social and Personal Relationships*,[1]

> people who started a new relationship quickly had higher well-being and a better opinion of themselves compared to those who waited longer to begin their subsequent relationship. Because of their fairly rapid transition between partners, rebounding individuals had less time with the single status and so their degree of well-being and self-esteem may have been less affected. In other words, their relatively uninterrupted relationship status may have allowed their lifestyle to flow more smoothly over this period of time and thus the breakup may have had fewer global effects on their psychological health.

Nonetheless, I think it's essential to resist the urge to jump into any kind of relationship quickly. If it happens too early, even if it's just for "fun," you may be opening up wounds that haven't fully healed yet—for both your kids and you. Children take a long time to understand and trust a new situation, so if you step into a rebound relationship that is likely to fail, your child will feel even more scared, insecure, and unsafe. And they will inevitably act out. This is when substance abuse, academic decline, and poor decision making come into play.

---

1 Claudia C. Brumbaugh and R. Chris Fraley, "Too Fast, Too Soon?: An Empirical Investigation into Rebound Relationships," *Journal of Social and Personal Relationships* 32, no. 1 (2015): 99–118, http://journals.sagepub.com /doi/pdf/10.1177/0265407514525086.

When your child concludes that your coupling off again is even an option, it can be quite unsettling to think about, let alone having them be aware that it's already happening or seeing it with their own eyes. Keep in mind that even if your kids say they just want you to be happy, your happiness with someone else will likely inversely correlate with how safe and secure they feel. Kids also don't want a new parental figure, no matter who it is.

Boundaries, Not Burdens

You and your ex need to navigate not only custody issues and new parenting dynamics as your family evolves but also your relationship with each other. Do whatever it's going to take—no matter how painful or uncomfortable—to morph your dissolved marriage into a new, functional, peaceful partnership. Not because you want to but because you *have* to. You *must* get along. You need to create an alliance with your former partner and both clearly communicate how you want your new relationship to look. The more you can set ground rules and expectations, the better it will be for your kids, so consider sitting down with a psychiatrist or therapist to help you in this endeavor.

A big part of what you'll need to zero in on will be boundaries. The saying that good fences make good neighbors is true; even if the two of you live nowhere near each other, you'll need clearly defined boundaries. For example, you used to be able to ask questions of your ex that may no longer be appropriate to ask, even as you remain coparents. A rule of thumb is to stay away from asking questions that have to do with sex or money or that draw parallels to or remind you of your old relationship. It's natural to want to know what's going on with your ex—if they're dating someone, how they're parenting, what they're doing daily, and more. But you cannot, under any circumstances, put your child in a position to talk about what's going on in the other household. It will crush your child's understanding of trust, loyalty, and honesty, and it will cause major emotional and mental problems in the long run. Even seemingly innocuous questions such as "Who put you to bed?" or "Did Mommy feed you lunch?" can feel to your kids like they're caught in a tug-of-war. Whether you try to do it subtly or your questions are obviously intrusive, your kids are not stupid and they know when they're being grilled. They shouldn't be in a position that could get their other parent in "trouble," that makes them feel like by responding with basic facts they are in fact tattling, or that makes them fearful that their other parent will be skewered thanks to them.

Likewise, do not expect your child to withhold information from their other parent or burden them with information they shouldn't have. I have a patient, a young boy, who is currently keeping a secret from his mother: his father is seeing his mother's close friend. That kind of secrecy weighs heavily on a child, because they are put in a position to be an emotional guardian for the people who are supposed to be theirs. What an unfair burden.

It takes time to adapt to the new boundaries of your evolved relationship. As you morph out of your old life and into a new one, you will definitely experience growing pains. It's not easy, and it's no small feat to shield your kids from the struggles along the way. But the more you and your ex treat each other with respect and put your kids' needs first, the smoother this process will be. When your family evolves, you still have every opportunity to give your children what they need most. It takes time, self-awareness, and work, but their sense of permanence and safety will remain intact, or become stronger than ever, if they are your highest priority at all times along your journey as an evolving family navigating complicated dynamics.

Staying United as Families Blend

When the time is right, if you have a new long-term relationship, you'll need to clearly define that person's role with your ex and with your children. For example, if your children have a stepparent, does everyone understand that both biological parents will take the lead, and the stepparent will follow suit? Let's get specific. If Johnny's mother says no to his request for a skateboard, and then Johnny turns to his stepdad with the same request, rather than undermining his wife to gain favor with his stepson, the appropriate response should be "Let me talk to your mother"—even if he instinctively wants to buy it. Children need to see their biological parent and a new partner as united or else they will play them off each other, just as they will do between exes if they see that the parental figures can't work as a unit.

You must establish the adult-to-child relationship between stepparent and stepchild. In general, stepparents try to enter the situation by being fun and generous so the new children like them, but inevitably that backfires. You must make sure that your new partner is respected and acting respectful. If the stepparent tries too hard to be liked, your child will not learn to respect them and will eventually learn to lose respect for you based on the partner you've chosen. On the flip side, if the new stepparent tries to assert too many of their own rules, the kids may reject the new standards as not being part of the family portrait. They should be an ally and supporter of the stepchild, but understand that it will take time to build a close relationship. Trust that their relationship will take its own path. Often biological parents put pressure on their child to like the new partner, but that usually leads to the opposite. Allow their relationship to grow without pushing it on either of them. By putting no pressure on this relationship, you'll give your child the opportunity to learn to like your new partner on their own. You'll be easing your new partner into your child's life as well.

The new stepparent must support the relationship between stepchild and the other biological parent, should never give opinions on the other parent, and should be a neutral person who does not choose sides. Again, make sure your new partner is not trying to be a friend to your child. They are not. Their job is to listen, not give parenting opinions around your child, and to take their cues from your and your ex-partner's parenting.

If you and your ex-partner are still cordial, your new partner should try to connect with your ex-partner. In doing so they will create a level of trust between them, and in your suggestion of this, you're showing a respect for your ex-partner that will be reciprocated. Think about it: wouldn't you want to know everyone interacting with your children? I find it helpful to have a sit-down, just the two of them, to get to know each other. Building a healthy relationship between the two of them is something that will help to ensure a seamless parenting process in this new evolution of your relationship. If you and your ex are not cordial, and there is no possibility of growing this new relationship, then the new partner should simply follow your lead and lay low. If your child ever approaches your new partner with questions or opinions about your family system, make sure your new partner listens but doesn't share opinions.

I worked with a couple that was together for fifteen years and had three children, ages ten, eight, and three. They separated after the husband had had an affair, fallen in love with the woman, and then ultimately moved in with her. You can imagine how hurt the ex-wife was, and how hard it was for her when he asked for 50 percent custody. I urged the mother of these children to let them see their father, and, more important, to let them love him, even though she hated him and wanted nothing to do with him. I had a meeting with the father and mother, and we hashed out a very deliberate plan for how the children would meet their father's new live-in girlfriend.

At first the children only saw her as one of his friends. They would meet her as part of a group in order to dilute the intensity of their interactions. Slowly and methodically, she met them amid smaller and smaller groups of friends, until it was just her, the children, and their dad. Once a level of comfort had developed between the children and this new woman, their father could then tell them that she was more than a friend.

Throughout this time, I met regularly with the mother to dissolve and resolve her anger and ensure that her children remained her focus. By the time her children were meeting with her ex-husband's new partner and she had dealt with her negative feelings and heartbreak, I set up a meeting between her and her ex's new partner. They got to talk about the kids, how they should be treated, how to create some consistency, and how they would communicate. It wasn't pleasant, but it was cordial.

Even though it's unpleasant, it *can* work. Once the kids knew that everything was friendly (enough) among all parties, they could take a breath. The goals are *their* safety and feelings of permanence, right? Never lose sight of those. If you are already in a blended family with children from both parents, you must be cognizant of treating all children the same, even though you will probably feel more connected to your biological children. Your biological children will likely struggle when they see the family evolving to include new members, especially if those are other kids. But everyone has to be held to that standard or it's not going to work. As early in the process as you can, create a new family portrait with your blending family, where everyone has a chance to discuss and contribute toward the values, expectations, and priorities of the new makeup. By keeping everyone on the same playing field, and not straying from it, all the confusion and feelings of discombobulation will eventually subside, and you'll become a united family.

No matter where you are on the path of your family's evolution, your changing family is an opportunity to pull together with your coparent to become the team your children need. Behavior speaks louder than words, so show your children that you are a united front that can rise above any grievances to coparent successfully. Even when you disagree, work to become a team in discipline, setting boundaries, giving consequences, talking about their strengths, navigating social issues, and more. There's no such thing as quitting here. Your family values are in your hands even when—*especially* when—your family evolves.

CHAPTER 13

Lightning Round of Common Questions

Obviously I wasn't there with you in the hospital when you became a parent, but I feel pretty confident that nobody handed you a parenting handbook on that fateful day that could successfully address every parenting situation you'll be faced with. I'm also pretty sure you haven't received a full-proof parenting bible of sorts in the years since. That doesn't exist, of course, because there's no one-size-fits-all approach on parenting different personalities, navigating complex dynamics, and keeping your family intact and thriving on the heels of a life-disrupting pandemic. Nonetheless, throughout my three decades working with families across the country, I have seen similar themes and questions arise, so that's where this chapter, filled with frequently asked questions, comes in. You'll also find some of the more recent questions parents have been asking in light of the pandemic and our changing world. Of course, every family and situation is different, so I recommend that you consult with an expert about your specific experience.

Q: What do I do if my kid is lying?

A: I hope that you have laid the foundation by both your role-modeling and face-to-face conversations with your children that lying has no place in your home. If your kids hear you canceling plans saying you're under the weather when in fact you just got a better offer, you have not. So look inward at what you're modeling for your kids, and how clear the example you set is of when white lies are okay, when you need to bend the truth to fit your needs, and when you hide information or keep secrets from the people in your life to spare their feelings or reduce your own discomfort. Because no matter how pure your intentions are, your kids are always watching.

To some degree, lying is typical for most children. A child might lie to get attention, to avoid getting in trouble, to minimize discomfort in a particular situation, or because they're embarrassed. When you find yourself in a position where your child is lying to you, how you react will dictate if they do it again, including how often and to what degree. The higher the volume of your reaction, the higher the chances that your child continues to lie. In other words, rather than raising your voice or responding with outrage, you should have an age-appropriate discussion about why they lied, why it's not the right thing to do, and how to conscientiously undo any damage that the lie has caused. Younger children may not yet understand the concept of morality tied to lying, while older children are presenting you with a teachable moment when they're "caught." If your child's lying is a new development that you're noticing, it's possible that it's a red flag you need to be attentive to, because the roots may lie elsewhere and could be problematic. As with all potential red flags, you may need to be ready to investigate where this is coming from and how serious it is. Focus on building a rapport with your child, teaching right vs. wrong, and understanding what the underlying motivation was for their lie rather than harping on a consequence or punishment. Work together to fix the problem of whatever they were lying about in a calm and respectful manner. These are investments you'll need to model and work on for years to come; it's a practice that should take you to a good place until you send them off to college with integrity.

Q: Does it work to give my child a time-out or ground them? Do you have a spectrum of punishments or consequences that work?

A: The usual consequences of a time-out or grounding need to be understood as methods of punishment that only make your child angry with you, incentivizing them to become more manipulative, sneaky, and rebellious. In other words, such consequences are often ineffective in achieving the outcome parents want. Even as your child complies with your time-out or grounding, they're sitting there stewing, stirring up more anger and resentment within themselves, which I can guarantee will surface in the weeks to come, bringing you right back where you started.

If your teen has blown through his curfew or your younger child has acted out in an inappropriate or harmful way, there are better reactions than a punishment. Use their behavior as an opportunity to teach them *how* and *why* to eradicate the behavior that created the situation. Calmly engage in an age-appropriate dialogue with your child. Talk about how they could better handle the same circumstances in the future. All too often, parents become emotional (as is understandable), during the child's acting out. However, logic is the only real way to make headway and ultimately eradicate the negative behaviors that got your child into this dialogue with you. Let them take ownership of their behavior and work together to handle any aftermath of their behavior so they feel your support and gain the tools to behave differently in the future.

Q: I've done all the work on my side but my kid is still acting out. How do I discipline them?

A: If you've done "all the work," it would mean you not only have self-awareness about your role, but also understand your child's needs and have insight about why they don't feel solid, which then leads to their acting out. If that has truly been done properly, then the need to discipline should be minimized or become nonexistent. That's how you know you've done "all the work." So if you're asking this question, then you are among the many people who also ask it when they have not fully committed to doing the work.

I'm here to tell you that if you truly do the work, you'll see the payoff. Some parents think this will be a much easier goal to reach than it really is, and once they get started they may get discouraged. Take a look at the seemingly minor but positive steps you have made as a parent and as a family. There is no such thing as a small success because each and every success implemented by you is a huge one. So make sure you're taking the time to congratulate yourself and enjoy the benefits of your hard work. You can also celebrate these successes as a family. Once you've made your SWEEP road map, for example, display it where it can be seen throughout the day so that all family members can look and track progress. Seeing it every day is very motivating for all families, but especially for those families that have a longer way to go to reach their goals. It's also important that each family member has a chance to voice their feelings and their thoughts regarding this process. Age-appropriate dialogue is an excellent option at all times, except when your child is acting out, hungry, or tired. Perhaps during mealtime once or twice a week, everyone can casually check in about how they're feeling regarding their progress individually and as a family.

I also want you to understand that you're supposed to feel frustrated, at times even defeated and inclined to give up. That's normal, because this work is hard! It wouldn't be so darn worth it if it weren't. When you get to this place, identify how you feel and know it's a sign for you and your parenting partner to support each other even more rather than to give in to the discomfort or throw in the towel altogether. If you do the latter, you'll be letting yourself and your family down. So start slowly time and time again and appreciate every gain you make rather than overwhelming yourself with wanting huge change quickly. Your family didn't get to this place overnight, and it will take time—coupled with patience, love, and respect—to get to where you want and need to be.

Q: Why does my child get so angry with me when my response to a request is "Maybe"?

A: Children are concrete thinkers. What that means is they think in terms of yes/no, so when you give a response such as "maybe" or "not sure," the lack of clarity gets them upset. Your child is looking for an answer that's "black" or "white," so when your response is "gray" they feel confused, uncertain, and in turn can get out of sorts. So "no" means "no" and "yes" means "yes." Get rid of the "maybe."

Q: Is it okay to look at my kid's phone/social media accounts/ email if I think they're doing something they shouldn't? Do I need to tell them before I do?

A: The moment your child gets a phone and/or social media, they need to understand the ground rules that you may check it at any time. None of us wants our privacy invaded, no matter how old we are, so be up front that scrolling through their feeds, text messages, or the like is not a violation of their privacy. If you don't tell your child the terms of this privilege— yes, it's a privilege—from the get-go, their perception of your checking up on them could be a wound that can cut deeply and damage your relationship for many years to come. That would lead to many more problems than you ever thought you had.

Consider creating a social media or tech contract clearly spelling out that it's very much within your rights to look at their exchanges. You both should sign this contract as an indication that expectations are very clear and so you can refer to the document going forward. The best outcome when giving your child technology is that there are no surprises. Make random spot checks of whatever facet you want to see a condition for getting social media or new technology. Consider making a term be that you are allowed to follow them on social media and read their comments—part of the deal can be that you're not allowed to comment yourself or otherwise "embarrass" your child. Before allowing your child access to the privilege, make clear what your expectations are for how they conduct themselves and what the consequences are if those expectations or any of the other terms of the contract are violated. When you set up a very clear code of conduct, you are better positioned to remain an authority figure if and when issues do arise.

You should not wait until your child does something that you're suspicious of before you start checking. Your child's safety should supersede any right to privacy you may think they have. Is your child, who can easily become a target of a predator or a victim of online abuse, equipped to protect themselves? Trust me, they're not. Their neurological development is not at a place for them to be able to have the judgment or the insight to know when a situation may be dangerous, especially online. That's your job as a parent, so it's well within your rights to look.

Q: What do I do if my child will not allow me to follow them on their Instagram or other social media accounts?

A: This is a perfect example of what should be clearly spelled out in your tech contract with your child. If following your child on social media is important to you, then have that indicated in the contract when they are first allowed to have social media. Doing it later is very difficult, especially if you have an established and very trusting and respectful relationship with your child. But if that is where you find yourself, just remember that it is never too late. Have an honest conversation with your child about the need for a change, and explain the parameters of what needs to be different. Introduce a code of conduct and make clear what the consequences are of not fulfilling it. It likely will be uncomfortable at the onset, especially if your child is used to digital independence, but you are the parent and it's your call.

Q: Is it safer to let my kids drink in the house rather than risk them sneaking out to drink?

A: The primary issue here should not be about whether you allow your kids to drink at home to prevent them from sneaking out. The issues, as I see it, are these: Have you established the relationship you need to have with your children or teens to be able to have an open and honest dialogue regarding substance use? Have you role-modeled a responsible relationship with alcohol for your kids? Do they hear you and your partner saying, "Which one of us can drink tonight so the other can drive home safely?" In general, when driving isn't involved, do they see you cut yourself off after one cocktail so you can get to work on time and be at your best the next day? In terms of allowing your child to drink at home, I understand that you don't want your child to sneak it or be in a more unsafe position when driving or when other external factors come into play, but the message you're sending when underage drinking happens in your home is that it's okay to break the law. Despite the rationalization a parent may use to allow their teen to drink at home, statistics have shown it is a very dangerous slope with multiple bad outcomes.

Q: I found drugs in my kid's bag. What do I do?

A: No matter whether what you found is a prescription drug or a street drug such as weed, cocaine, fentanyl, heroin, or anything else, your discovery must be taken seriously. Confiscation of those drugs is your first step, followed by a logical—not emotional—discussion. Depending on the extent of the substance use and the underlying issues that the drugs were being used to self-medicate, an appropriate plan should be made and implemented. You may need to involve the police or other officials as you uncover more about how your child obtained the drugs and the other circumstances involved. I should point out that your child may not even be taking the drugs; he could be selling them or giving them to friends—which is a crime called underage drug dealing. It's critical that every member of your family understands that there are consequences to breaking rules, and those consequences extend to breaking laws. Covering for your child or negotiating with them to keep it in the family makes you an accomplice and an enabler—it's as simple and straightforward as that. There's no reason your child should have drugs of any sort that you aren't aware of, even if they were given to them for an appropriate medical reason.

A common denominator for many teens who use drugs is that they're self-medicating, sometimes for ADHD, anxiety, conduct disorder, or oppositional defiant disorder, whether diagnosed or undiagnosed. They may think it feels good in the moment, but it inevitably takes them down a dark path. Many kids who use drugs also have a significant family history of mental health and substance abuse. Oftentimes there are unaddressed issues at home that the child is struggling with, and drugs are an escape or a quick fix that allows them to disconnect from the challenges that are out of their control. As unfortunate as this is, you may have missed red flags along the way before discovering the drugs. I say that not to blame you but because all parents need to be on the lookout for red flags like drugs, including parents who think "My child would never do drugs! Not a chance!" No parent wants to find out that drugs are a part of their child's life, but it's a real possibility, so you need to be looking for red flags and be as prepared as possible to jump into action.

When you speak with your child about what you found, remember to use a 50 percent head and 50 percent heart formula so you can have a dialogue that's calm, respectful, and honest. You need to find out everything you can about the substances you found, how often your child has been using them, and for how long. As you gather information about what led your child down this path, you'll also want to SWEEP your child; set up an appointment for a physical exam, including bloodwork; and implement changes such as curfews or no technology until more clarity and understanding is received. As upsetting as this is, remember to be patient during this process; getting incredibly angry will only contribute to their possible shame, pain, anger, or resentment, or whatever emotions are at play for your struggling child. If you get out of control, you'll be adding fuel to the fire that your child is attempting to cope with—or to avoid coping with—by using drugs.

Q: My child is bigger than I am, and I'm afraid of them getting physical with me. How am I supposed to discipline them?

A: If you're afraid of your own child, then you have allowed them to hold way too much power for probably far too long. Depending on your circumstances, you may actually be at a place now where outside forces need to intervene—for example, if your child has been fighting at school, or intimidating someone outside of school. It's best to use logic and respect to get them to engage with you. But if you genuinely feel unsafe around your child, then it's time to call in reinforcements. Make clear to your child that you're willing to escalate by calling Child Services or even the police if they cannot or will not reduce the physical threat— and then, if they don't, you must be ready to make the call. It's your responsibility to keep your home a safe place.

Q: How do I know if my child has suffered from the pandemic?

A: The best way to know if your child has suffered on any level from the pandemic is to be aware of how they function by doing a SWEEP of them. From that you can gather information about many key areas of your child's life and address the ones that seem to be of concern to you.

Q: Is telling my teenager they will be randomly drug tested upon returning home from being out with their friends a good thing to do?

A: It's important to understand that a relationship must be nourished and built with your child that has respect, open communication, trust, and honesty as the foundations. If those foundations are in place, then at the appropriate age when your child is venturing out into the world socially with their friends, it is appropriate to have an open discussion with honesty and respect about your expectations regarding substances. In that discussion, it can be appropriate to introduce the concept of random drug testing upon return to home.

If, however, that relationship is not present between you and your child before the teenage years, then introducing random drug testing may be seen as a scare tactic that leads to mistrust between the two of you as well as dishonesty from your child. It's never too late to work on building the relationship, so you're in a solid place to have a discussion along those lines.

Q: My child says that he "wants to die" when he gets angry or we say no to something he really wants. It frightens me but I'm not sure he means it. What should I do?

A: Whenever a parent hears that their child wants to die, it must be taken seriously. You need to reach out to your doctor, mental health provider, or any hotline you may have access to so you can talk to a professional who will guide you. If your child is saying they want to die as a form of manipulation, that will be dealt with after the initial assessment needed for the seriousness of their suicidality.

When a child is evaluated, they may see many different mental health professionals, but ultimately an assessment is done by a psychiatrist, preferably a child or adolescent psychiatrist. This can be a very difficult time for many families because it becomes very real that you, your child, and your family may be at a point of a crisis. The medical professionals are there to help you, and I encourage you to ask questions and be completely honest as you work together to gain clarity on the situation and assess next steps.

In addition to speaking with you, the evaluator will likely assess your child alone to understand any issues leading to your child verbalizing and feeling suicidal. The professional will ask very specific questions regarding their thoughts and feelings about suicide, including how long they have felt this way, if they're aware of anything that may have triggered this feeling, if they've had this feeling before, and if they truly want to die. They will also be asked if they have a plan and if they have access to items with which they can implement their plan. For example, do they have access to a rope, a gun, or a knife?

This is obviously a very emotional time, so I recommend that you take notes you can refer to when things calm down. Once the evaluator has spoken to all those whom they feel are important sources of information, a decision will be made about the appropriate next steps to keep your child safe.

Q: I've noticed a pattern of when my child has a tantrum or an outburst. Once they calm down, they are usually starving. What does that mean?

A: As a medical doctor, I always make sure before diagnosing a patient with any mental health disorder that they are medically cleared. That means they have a physical and bloodwork to make sure no medical problems are presenting themselves in any mental health fashion; make sure these procedures and tests are done. It seems as if low blood sugar may account for some of your child's tantrums. especially since they're hungry after and irritated and angry before. Hypoglycemia can make anyone feel irritable and angry, so be sure your child has the appropriate nutrition regularly each day and see if that will get rid of or at least reduce some of this negative behavior.

Q: My child seems to be very sad and depressed. How do I know if they need medication?

A: Whenever you have any questions or concerns about your child from a mental health perspective, especially whether they would benefit from medication, it's important that you seek out the appropriate professional to do an extensive assessment before any treatment or medication is pursued. For children, a board-certified child and adolescent psychiatrist is the place to go with any of your mental health concerns. They will do the evaluation needed to answer all your questions and put a treatment plan in place that may include medication for your child.

Most recently many pediatricians are taking added training to be qualified as developmental pediatricians. Using this professional as an alternative may not always be what is best for your child. Your insurance company may require you to start with your pediatrician or your general family doctor and then get a referral to a psychiatrist. Whatever channels you must go through to reach the specialist, it will be well worth it.

Q: What does it mean when you say "respect your child"?

A: Just because their child is younger than their parents doesn't mean respect is not a critical part of the relationship. I'm here to tell you that they deserve and require respect; when they don't get it or feel it, they may not be able to tell you, but they will definitely show you that they don't like it. Parents need to respect their children by being on time to pick them up or drop them off, following through with commitments they've made previously, giving them honest answers even when the truth is difficult, and talking to them and handling them in a calm, respectful manner no matter what the issue is. All of these are ways to show your child that you respect them while at the same time remaining a parent who will discipline and guide your child into adulthood.

Q: Do I need to worry if my child is being socialized enough if he's online with his friends playing games?

A: Unfortunately, the pandemic has allowed our children to live even more of their life online. Although they may have friends online that they're interacting with through gaming or other means, that is hardly a substitute for the in-person socialization that all our children need. So yes, if your child is now choosing to remain online more than in person from a social perspective, you do need to worry and you need to fix that.

If your child has unfortunately become too comfortable remaining online and is resisting in-person socialization, please see that as a red flag. You need to slowly reintegrate your child, working them through whatever social anxiety or separation anxiety emerges as they venture from your home. Helping them understand what is happening, what they are feeling, and why they are feeling it will be key to supporting them through it. Once they reach the other side and begin to socialize, they will see and quickly remember the benefits they once had being with their friends. If you continue to meet resistance with your child, you may want to seek the help of a mental health professional or discuss it with your doctor, because your child may need a professional approach to address their anxiety barrier.

Q: My kids are less academically inclined since the pandemic. It started when their school went online, and they never got their motivation back. Any advice for how to reignite a passion for learning and get caught up?

A: Many parents are seeing this, unfortunately. It's an epidemic within the epidemic, as kids are less motivated academically and socially and have critical gaps in their education. The data showing the specifics of the regression that happened for our children when they weren't in the classroom is just starting to surface. If you have the opportunity or means to support and supplement your children's education yourself or with outside resources, that may be beneficial. However, if your child is truly unmotivated, your first order of business is to reignite the desire to learn. If you remember how your kids were pre-pandemic as far as their learning and motivation levels, try to pinpoint precisely how they've changed post-pandemic so you know which aspects of their education need the most attention. Start with a SWEEP so you can gather information not only about their education but also about other areas of their life that could be impacting them in school. This is a critical starting point from which to address your child's needs and reignite their interest in life in general, and specifically their education.

Q: Coparenting is hard, and so is marriage! What are the biggest differentiators between marriages that last and those that don't?

A: From my perspective, it comes down to simple tools of communication. If a person comes to the dating table knowing how to communicate effectively and respectfully (tools that were role modeled by their parents, as you now understand), they're starting a relationship light-years ahead of someone who doesn't know how to communicate effectively, calmly, respectfully, and with the give–and–take that relationships require. That said, these tools can be taught and implemented by anyone who's willing to do the work of learning and controlling their interactions with their partner. The key here is that they must want to do it. When that's the case, then those marriages make it into the survival category. As soon as couples begin to slip or slide, communication is essential, and I include emotional and physical intimacy as a critical subset of that communication. When times get tough in a marriage (or any relationship), approaching your partner from a loving place coupled with mastery of kind and effective communication will help you make it through the storm.

At the end of every day—that's right, I mean daily— you need to let go of any hurt, anger, fear, insecurity, and resentment between you and your partner, particularly on days when your communication has been subpar, or your marriage will pay a steep price.

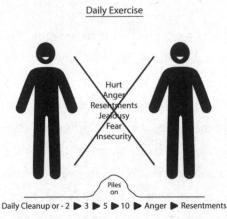

Daily Exercise

Q: When a crisis arises, what's a common mistake you see families make?

A: I see families divide to conquer, which they should never do. There's no room for criticism, fault, or incrimination in times of crisis. Doing that will only misguide and distract you. Even if it's one family member who's the impetus for the issues you're experiencing, you must try to band together as a family. There's no time or energy for being cynical, pointing fingers, or taking cheap shots at anyone. As a leader of your family, you must support your team members no matter how you feel; that's the only way to come out the other side stronger and with your family unit intact. If you have a coparent, you each need clearly defined roles based on your individual strengths. I also see emotions running high in some families. While that's understandable, it's not particularly helpful. The only way to see clearly in high-pressure situations is to control your emotions and remain calm. That's why I suggest that parents "unhook and take a look" so they can drop their temperature and be prepared to communicate with 50 percent head and 50 percent heart, as opposed to an imbalance such as 80 percent emotion and 20 percent logic.

Q: If you could get parents to change just one thing to improve their families, what would it be?

A: I would ask them to role-model for their children the kind of person they would like their child to become. Are you living in a way that's congruent with the family values that you proclaim to hold dear and want your children to live in accordance with? So many times I hear parents lament that they don't like the people their children are becoming. It's possible you're seeing the qualities in your kids that you like least about yourself. So look in the mirror, dig deep about where you've been and where you are now, and make the necessary changes for both you and your children. With SWEEP as your foundational structure, you can even role-model in your sleep! Seriously, your role-modeling starts with SWEEP and expands to include every aspect of your life. You are your children's most powerful role model, period.

CONCLUSION

Meet Jolene, a fourteen-year-old in ninth grade living with her parents and three older siblings. Academically, she had always been an average student and was minimally involved in extracurricular activities or outside interests. She had no problem making friends; in fact, she was often the one starting group texts and sharing funny TikTok videos in the chat. The first red flag her parents noticed was that Jolene had stopped posting on social media, which had been a daily routine for her. It was just a subtle change, and a somewhat positive one at that, but noticeable nonetheless.

In the spring semester of ninth grade, Jolene started to show significant academic improvement. Her parents were quite pleased, and assumed she was just maturing and taking school more seriously as she began to understand how high school grades could impact her future. Jolene was also hanging out with a new friend group, teenagers her parents weren't as familiar with. Perhaps, they thought, these friends were a good influence, so they gave Jolene more independence as she navigated her freshman year.

There's nothing more powerful than a parent's intuition, and Jolene's mom listened to hers by asking for a consultation with me.

She had a nagging feeling that she shouldn't take her daughter's newfound academic success, reduced use of social media, and new friend group at face value. She had also noticed that her daughter seemed to need less sleep, which we confirmed as soon as I taught Jolene's parents how to SWEEP the whole family. When they came back with their findings a few weeks later, everyone's SWEEP was in pretty good shape. I did, however, take note that Jolene's sleep was erratic. By our third session, we noticed that her appetite was off and her sleep cycle was further disrupted, even though, interestingly, her schoolwork was still improving. Those red flags were what prompted me to meet with Jolene one on one.

Jolene and I talked about the changes in her SWEEP. She had many reasons for the alterations, including her recent academic success, but to me, they didn't all add up. I sent her for a physical exam, including blood work. I was specifically looking for a medical issue that could mask itself and present as a mental health issue, such as thyroid disease, anemia, or other medical concerns that needed to be taken out of the equation before I could dig further. I also had Jolene do a battery of psychoeducational testing to assess her strengths and needs and to ensure that her learning environment was suitable.

One morning a few months into her second semester, Jolene forgot her backpack at home. She called her mom and asked if she would drop it off at school. When her mom picked up the backpack, which wasn't completely zipped up, out fell a vape pen. Jolene's mom had no idea what it was, but a quick search on the internet got her up to speed on how kids ingest nicotine these days. She dropped the backpack off at school without mentioning her findings.

That afternoon, after gathering their thoughts and preparing a working script for speaking with their teen, Jolene's parents sat down with her. They learned that Jolene had been using nicotine since winter break, when one of her friends offered her their vape pen to try. Jolene noticed that she felt better when using it; she described herself as more focused, attentive, and happier overall since she'd started vaping. Jolene managed to get someone to purchase one for her, and she began to use it on a daily basis. Both parents were confused as to why Jolene had turned to vaping, but admitted they understood why she felt it was beneficial to her.

The next time we all met, I got a thorough update from Jolene and her parents about all that had transpired. Because I had a few rounds of SWEEPs to look at and a better understanding of the evolution of the behavior, I was able to see that the improvement in Jolene's schoolwork and overall happiness were indeed connected to the vaping. Nicotine is a stimulant, and stimulants such as nicotine, Ritalin, or Adderall are used to treat disorders of attention such as ADD and ADHD. What Jolene had stumbled on without even being aware of it herself was a way to self-medicate issues she'd been having with focus and attention. I explained to the family that stimulants work in the opposite way with people who have a hard time concentrating, giving them increased focus and reduced restlessness. Once we understood the impact that the nicotine was having on Jolene, we were able to then pursue a course to find her a healthy treatment plan. Her medical workup showed that there were no issues of concern, but her psychoeducational testing led to a diagnosis of ADHD. We worked with the school to make learning accommodations, and Jolene's parents were able to provide her with additional outside support to assist with organizational and executive functioning. I consequently gave Jolene a prescription for a stimulant and advised her to discontinue all use of nicotine. I commended Jolene's mom for listening to her gut when even seemingly minor red flags were raised, because Jolene's addiction to nicotine could have escalated if it went unnoticed, creating more problems for her at a critical time in her development.

I urge you, too, to be on the lookout for red flags. There's a difference between "normal" teen behavior, for example, and a teen on the verge of crisis. You've got to emerge from complancency and pay attention to the subtle or not-so-subtle changes they're exhibiting so you can spot the red flags. No matter how old your children are, when you're actively listening, engaging in a meaningful way with open lines of communication, SWEEPing on a regular basis, behaving like a Balanced Parent, setting boundaries, role-modeling, and prioritizing your child's safety and permanence, you'll be able to overcome challenges with your family values intact—I'm sure of it. I'm also sure that no matter where you are on your parenting journey, it isn't too late to break cycles that are disruptive, to discard your baggage, to set new precedents, and to live in accordance with your most deeply held values. It's not too late for you, for your children, and for your family.

This is the hardest job you'll ever have, but you and I know that there's nothing in the world worth working harder for—and now more than ever, because the pandemic has given us a wake-up call we cannot ignore. For some people, Covid-19 has meant human loss, job loss, and home loss that rocked the family structure. If you weren't in a particularly good place before, you're likely in a much worse place now. Family structures that may have been on shaky ground to begin with are now teetering, and in many cases have collapsed. After enduring the unimaginable, we all have an opportunity to hit the reset button, to get on the same page about who we are and what really matters. The time for change is now; the tools are free, and they're in your hands.

I wrote this book because I want to help you and your family. I want you to have the tools to face tough parenting moments head-on and come out stronger; to see where you have room for growth and to set goals that you can achieve; to create the kind of family that you might have wished for as a child yourself; to believe that happiness and wholeness are yours to claim and work for; to dig deep to uncover the family values that will add immeasurable value to your life now and for generations to come. We need to change the way we engage with our kids, learn how to recognize red flags, and develop the skills our children need us to have so we can provide them with the security and permanence they need to thrive. The tools I've shared with you in these pages may seem basic or easy, but I assure you that they're transformative and essential. No matter what your family situation is right now, your situation will always improve when you take a closer look at how you provide that foundation for your children.

Just moments ago I was on a video call with a family whose son, a high school sophomore, has been so isolated throughout the pandemic that he's struggling to venture into the world once again. The parents lack self-control and self-knowledge, as well as awareness of the magnitude of what's at stake if they don't get out of denial and hit the reset button. Of course, they're not alone. Data show that we have left our children shattered in so many ways. As a child and adolescent psychiatrist, I'm incredibly distressed by the increased rates of abuse, neglect, isolation, anxiety, depression, and suicidality. As a physician and parent, I'm also concerned about our children's academic and professional futures, both at home and in comparison to their global peers, at a time when they've missed out on critical skill building and socialization. We're falling behind globally by numerous markers, drop-out rates are rising, and, after the pandemic has stolen more than two years from our children's lives, its aftermath is still not entirely clear.

It's been a perfect storm, and I desperately want to help. The call to action is urgent. The number of suicide attempts for children under age eighteen has skyrocketed. I alone have been putting young adults in rehab three or four times each month, so you can imagine how that shakes out when you think about our entire country. Every day I see more and more families slowly fragmenting and losing their way as their remaining family values erode to the point where they become unrecognizable or nonexistent.

Rich or poor, married or divorced, parent of one child or six, banker or farmer, left wing or right, Feather Parent or Tyrant Parent, workaholic or unemployed, child of loving parents or dysfunctional ones, gay or straight, in a decent place or in the midst of crisis . . . the message is the same no matter who you are, where you're coming from, or where you're headed. Parents are the solution to the problems destroying our children. That means you.

That sounds like a huge endeavor, but when you get down to it, what I'm asking of you—and what I hope you're asking of yourself—is discipline, commitment, and a willingness to do the work, which only you can accomplish. It seems so simple if you think about it, but I'll say it again: you wouldn't take a road trip without, at the very least, a sense of which direction you're headed in and where you hope to end up, so doesn't your most important entity—your family—deserve a road map and a plan? I hope I've not only convinced you how imperative that is but also incentivized you to take action.

A lot of families come to me feeling discouraged, frustrated, frightened, or exhausted—often all of the above. That is part of what makes the SWEEP tool I've created essential for you and your kids. If you don't know where to start, when you think you've gone too far off course, when you fear it's too late for you to turn things around, there's one tried and true place to begin: SWEEP. You can do it daily, weekly, monthly, or whatever feels right for you; whatever it takes to get a handle on what is going on with every member of your family. SWEEP gives you concrete goals to work on and a specific path to follow toward a healthier outcome for all of you. No matter what the next roadblock will be (and we all know there will be one), you'll be able to see around corners, get ahead of it, or tackle what hits by first and foremost having a strong foundation in place. I highly recommend a whiteboard as you chart your road map as a family, thinking of each other as the most important team you'll ever be on, your team for life.

As I see it, there's no true meaning to life without our family. What better reason do you need to seize this opportunity to build your family's values? Yes, I know, you're working your tail off to put a roof over your family's head, particularly in trying times, but every member of your family—including yourself—needs to have a clear understanding of how everyone is contributing to the happiness, growth, and success of the family. How about the infrastructure of your home, such as what you role model, how you communicate, building your children's sense of confidence, nurturing their education, connecting with one another, and supporting all the other critical pieces of their growth? I know you're busy. I am too, so I hear you. That's all the more reason why you need to stop in your tracks, take stock, and make sure that all of the work you are doing is fully aligned with the family values that define and resonate with each member of your family. I'm not saying that you should run your family like a bunch of robots consulting your whiteboard day in and day out (though that would certainly keep things clear and organized). But even the small changes we discussed in this book can have a life-changing impact on your kids by showing them that you are present, engaged, and genuinely able to express how much you care about them as individuals. Don't overwhelm yourself; just take one step at a time with commitment, consistency, and courage. I'm saying that I hope, for example, you'll now sit down with your family for dinner no matter how chaotic your life is and how many different directions you're all running in. Commit to eating together at least a few nights each week with everyone present, emotionally and physically. Family dinner is just one opportunity, but an important one, to hold one another accountable, diminish any resentment or anger that has built up, eradicate any hidden agendas, create more intimacy, and have fun together. I can guarantee you that the shift will happen, the shift that increases your family values in noticeable ways.

You're headed in the right direction by reading this book, but living out your family values is a process that requires ongoing commitment, passion, and patience. Even the smallest changes you make reap rewards. It becomes a circular process, a priceless gift, as living out your family values increases your family values—starting right now and lasting for generations to come.

ACKNOWLEDGMENTS

Throughout this book, you've heard me say time and time again that none of us should aim to be perfect. I certainly practice what I preach, both as a parent and as an author! I would first like to thank my son, Benjamin, for being in my life and providing me the wonderful opportunity to parent. Over time our relationship has evolved, struggled, and grown toward a healthy and stable parent and adult child relationship. Thank you for being patient over these last few years as this project came into sight and slowly coalesced into what it is today. There is no doubt that for the past nineteen years you've given me much joy, many tears, some sadness, and great pride, all of which have inspired me to use my experiences to inspire others.

In my role as an author, I'm thrilled to be far from "perfect," particularly because I'm supported by a team that is the absolute best in the industry. From our first FaceTime to our nine-millionth text message and post-midnight call, Rebecca Raphael, you are my secret weapon. (Not so secret anymore!) Thank you for using your profound talent with words to bring my voice and this book to life. I'm grateful for your tireless commitment, flexibility, and vision, and simply couldn't have asked for a better collaborator.

Leah Miller and the entire Simon Element team: Thank you for the opportunity to share my insights with readers everywhere, for your professionalism, and for your patience (I'm writing this in between patients—sorry it's late!). Your wisdom and support are the reason this book will help parents, children, and family units everywhere thrive.

I am exceptionally grateful to Jan Miller and her talented staff at Dupree Miller & Associates. Dr. Phil told me you were as good as they come, and you exceeded that by all measures. Your partnership got this project from the starting line to the finish line. Thank you.

Carla Pennington and the *Dr. Phil* show staff—I do not take for granted how fortunate I've been to be part of your TV family over the last decade, and am continually amazed at your ability to produce episode after episode that is compelling, authentic, well-researched, timely, and even life-changing. Thank you for adding my voice to your #1-rated show.

A very special thank-you to Dr. Phil McGraw, one of the most incredible role models, men, human beings, and best friends anyone could ask for. Thank you for your consistent love and support over these past fifteen years. You have allowed me to use my talents and experience, alongside yours, to influence and change the lives of so many people. I will always be grateful to you.

Last, thank you to all the parents and children who have welcomed me into your lives. I see you, I believe in you, and I hope that with this book, I will always be your partner in creating families and legacies that reflect your deepest-held *Family Values.*

INDEX

A

abandonment, feelings of, 42–43

academics. *See* school(s) and academics

acceptance, of your child, xix, 119–20, 122

active listening, 133–35, 144

Adderall, 227

addiction, 9, 13, 58, 227–28

ADHD/ADD, 213, 227

adolescents and teens. *See also* child(ren)

curfews for, 67–68

rise in depression and/or anxiety in, xiv

alcohol use, 212–13

American Psychological Association, 95

anger

emotional control and, 75

motivating your efforts, 21

anxiety

Covid-19 pandemic and social separation, 219–20

increase in incidence of, xiii, xiv

rise in adolescent, xiv

self-medication and, 213

undiagnosed learning disorder and, 160

apps, 177

arguments

about homework, 73

between parents, in front of the children, 11, 150

with your own parents, questions about, 46

authenticity, of family members, 119–20

authority. *See* power and power dynamics

B

baggage. *See* childhood experiences
(parent); family history;
unpacking and repacking
baggage
Balanced Parent, 76, 85–87
bedtime
getting enough sleep and, 96
lacking structure, 96
Tyrant Parent and, 77
behavior and changes in behavior
age of child and, 22
agreeing on targeted, 179
in Child Inventory, 33–34
making a list of desirable, 33–34
motivation and, 177–84
punishing versus talking about
inappropriate or harmful,
207–8
role-modeling and, 147–54
rules governing, in family
portrait, 115
self-inventory and, 28
blame, xx–xxi, 12, 37
blended families, 199–202
blood sugar levels, 98–99, 217–18
body language, 134, 136, 137,
139–40
boundaries
being progressive and, 127–28
consistency and, 67
curfews, 67–68
Feather Parent and, 81
importance of setting clear, 171

parent-child power dynamics
and, 55–56
Tyrant Parent and, 77, 80
with your ex-partner, 197–99
brain development
childhood experiences and, 14–15
child's access to money and, 60
trauma and, 74–75
bullying
increase in online, 103
loss of parental power and, 55–56

C

car, helping your child buy a, 172–73
celebrations, cultural, 124–26
celiac disease, 99
child(ren)
accepting individuality of, 119–22
backing away from, 53
brain development in, 14–15, 60,
74–75
collaboration with, 128
distressing situation of our,
229–30
drug use by, 213–14
exposing to different experiences,
120–21
fearing their parent, 75
grounding, 207–8
having a meaningful connection
with, 116–17
identifying behaviors and
attributes you would like to
see in, 33–34

influencing how you see your
parenting, 43–44

labels put on, 158–59

listening to, 133–35

looking at social media and
phone of, 210–11

loss of parental power to, 53–58

lying by, 206–7

motivating, 177–84

needs from parents, xviii–xix

in parental role, 9, 12–13

quality time spent with, 118,
194–95

questions asked to, 142, 162–63

resilience in, building, 164–65

respect for, 218–19

saying they "want to die,"
216–17

self-reflection on poor behavior
from your, 40–41

strengths of. *See* strengths

with a strong sense of culture,
124–26

time-outs for, 207–8

who do not feel they have control
over their lives, 158

Child Abuse Hotline, 52, 180

childhood experiences (parent). *See
also* family history; unpacking
and repacking baggage

asking yourself questions about
your, 40

healing from, 13–14

influence on parents, xiii, 9, 13

overcorrecting in response to our,
42–43, 77

parents understanding influences
from their, 14–17

repeating or avoiding aspects of,
40

child inventory, 33–34

Child Protective Services, 52, 73, 74

child welfare system, xi, 52–53, 60

choices, giving your child space to
make their own, 171–72

chores, 82, 176

code word or signal, used when
communicating, 134

collaboration with child(ren), 68, 128

communication, 133–44

about drug use, 216

about how and why to change
their behavior, 207–8

about power shift in the family,
63–65

about what will motivate your
child, 178–79

after finding drugs in your child's
bag, 214

asking your child questions,
162–63

by Balanced Parent, 86

body language and, 139, 140

conflicting internal messages and,
136–37, 139–40

at dinnertime, 142–43

emotional expression and, 101

humor and, 140–41

communication (*cont.*)
    listening to your child, 133–35, 144
    in marriages, 221–22
    positive self-talk and, 138–39
    proactive conversations, 127
    requirements for sender/receiver
        circle in, 135–37
    stepping back and unhooking
        during, 138
conduct disorder, 213
consequences
    boundaries having associated, 67
    grounding, 207–8
    motivating the child and, 181–82
    time-outs, 207–8
consistency
    boundary setting and, 67
    in enforcing rules, 82
    in helping your child discover
        their strengths and skills,
        163–64
    Seesaw Parent and, 84
    in spending time with your
        family, 118–19
    when regaining your parental
        power, 68
contracts
    curfew, 68
    technology/social media, 210, 211
coparenting, 193–95, 202, 221
Covid-19 pandemic, xiii, xiv
    adjusting to challenges of, 165
    determining if your child has
        suffered from, 215

    emotional health and, 102–3
    impact on family structure, 187,
        228
    impact on motivation for
        learning, 220–21
    impact on work life, 96–97
    in-person socialization and,
        219–20
    sleep and, 95
crises
    families being prepared for,
        187–88
    hanging your family portrait
        securely and weathering,
        126–28
    mistakes families make during,
        222–23
criticism, 121–22
crying, shift in power dynamics and,
    66
cultural traditions and connections,
    124–26
curfew contract, 68
curfews, 67–68
currency, 180, 181, 182–83
custody, 191–93, 194

D
depression
    in child, 218
    desire to play and, 106
    increase in incidence of, xiii,
        xiv
    in parents, 7

undiagnosed learning disorder
and, 160
developmental pediatricians, 218
dinners, family. *See* meals, families
sharing
dinnertime rituals, 142–43
disappointment, child's ability to
handle, 183
discipline. *See also* rules
Feather Parent and, 80, 81
having done "all the work" and,
208–9
parental power and, 61, 62
time-outs and grounding,
207–8
Tyrant Parent and, 80
when you feel unsafe with your
child, 215
dishonesty, 206–7
disrespect, 81, 150
divorce. *See* evolving families
divorce rate, 187
doctors. *See* medical doctor
drinking and driving, 212
Dr. Phil (television show), xvii
drugs, finding in your child's bag,
213–14
drug testing, 215–16

E
eating habits, 98–100, 108
emotional control, of parents, 75, 138
emotional expression
Covid-19 and, 102–3

improving your family's, 108
by parents, 100–101
emotional reactions
to child's academics, 160
shift in power dynamics and, 66
during times of crisis, 222–23
when communicating, 135
emotional safety, 10, 11, 30, 117, 136,
191
"emotional whiplash," 190
empathy, listening with, 135
EQ (emotional quotient), 97
evolving families
as better option for the parents
and the children, 188
boundaries with your ex in,
197–99
custody in, 191–93, 194
difference in coping and,
188–89
explained, 188
fundamental needs of, 189
parenting partnership in, 191–93
parents' emotional health and,
189
parents' role in, 189–91
parents working as a team in, 202
rebound relationships and,
195–97
exercises. *See also* self-inventory;
SWEEP
about your own parents, 44–46
answering questions about your
parenting, 43–44

exercises (*cont.*)
family portrait, 123–24
reframing the past, 40–42

F

family(ies). *See also* child(ren); parent(s)
eating meals together, 41–42,
100, 232
impact on later life of child, 15–16
making boundaries work for the
whole, 67–68
preparing for crises, 187–88
reported to child welfare system,
52–53
family history. *See also* childhood
experiences (parent);
unpacking and repacking
baggage
brain development and, 15
child's behavior triggering your
own, 40–41
of mental health and substance
abuse, 214
role-modeling and, 153
family identity, 114
family jokes, 122
family portrait
about, 113–15
accepting individuality of
members in your, 119–22
admiring the, 128–29
blended families and, 199, 202
cultural practices and customs in,
124–26

guiding principles of, 114–15,
122–24, 128–29
members feeling appreciated and
valued in, 115–16
prioritizing time spent together,
118–19
proactivity and progressiveness
in, 126–28
reminding children of, in
evolving families, 191
rules governing behavior in, 115
Family Power Questionnaire, 61–62
family projects, 143
family therapy, 58, 63
family values. *See* family portrait;
values
father(s). *See also* parent(s)
job loss, 7, 8, 13
not treated as an equal in
parenting, 59
projecting academic issues onto
son, 73–74
fear(s), 48, 54, 55, 75
Feather Parent, 80–84
firstborns, 9, 57
food(s) and eating, 98–100, 179
freedom to be a kid, child's need for,
xix
friend, children being their parent's,
189

G

gaslighting, 12
gluten intolerance, 99

grounding children, 207–8
guiding principles of the family,
     114–15, 122–24, 126, 128–29

H
high blood sugar, 98–99
hitting, 180
holistic approach to assessment,
     xii–xiii
home, letting your child drink at,
     212–13
home visits, 7–8
homework, 73, 82, 116
humor
     about power imbalances, 55
     communication and, 140–41
hunger, after a tantrum, 217–18
hybrid model of parenting, 39–40, 43
hyperglycemia, 98–99
hypoglycemia, 218

I
Identified Patient (IP), 11–13, 54, 57,
     67
independence, parental supervision
     and, 82–83
individuality, in the family, 115, 119
Instagram, parent following child on,
     211–12
instincts, listening to your, 25
interests, nurturing and encouraging
     your child's, 104, 121–22,
     161–64
intermittent currency, 183

interruption, speaking without,
     133–34
IQ (intelligence quotient), 97

J
job loss, 7, 8
jokes, family, 122
joking around, communication and,
     140–41
*Journal of Social and Personal
     Relationships*, 196
judgment, 119–20

L
labels, 158–61
laughing with versus at your child, 141
law, breaking the
     drinking at home and, 212
     finding drugs in your child's bag
          and, 213
learning (process)
     Covid-19's impact on motivation
          for, 220–21
     focus on, versus on rewards,
          159–60
     modeling an enthusiasm for, 161,
          162
     online, 97
     providing opportunities for your
          child's, 161–62
     struggles with, 160–61
lens
     examining your childhood
          through a different, 44–48

lens (*cont.*)
    your child's influence on your,
        43–44
listening to your child, 133–35, 144
Los Angeles County Department of
        Children and Family Services
        (DCFS), xi–xii
love
    acceptance of child and, xix
    expressing to your child, 101
    giving child money as an act of, 60
    power erosion and parent's need
        for child's, 56
    your parents' language of, 44
low blood sugar, 98, 217–18
lying, 206–7

M
marijuana use, 5–7, 11
marriages
    child's power and, 59
    communication in, 221–22
    emotional expression and, 108
    failed. *See* evolving families
    percentage ending in divorce, 188
mask wearing, impact of, 102
"maybe" responses, by parents, 210
meals, families sharing, 41–42, 63,
        100, 108, 142–43
medical doctor
    developmental pediatricians, 218
    social/separation anxiety and,
        220
    SWEEP and, 106

medical issues
    celiac disease, 99
    low blood sugar, 98, 217–18
medical marijuana, 5
mental health
    child appearing sad/depressed
        and, 218
    child saying they "want to die"
        and, 216–17
    Covid-19 pandemic and, 102
    drug use and, 212–13
    social/separation anxiety, 219–20
mistakes, 160
money, power and, 59–60
mother, substance abuse issues of,
        8–9
motivating your child, 177–84
motivation for learning, 220–21

N
negotiations with child(ren)
    benefits of understanding healthy
        ways of, 174–75
    everyday nonconfrontational
        ways of, 175
    honoring points of all family
        members and, 175–76
    in many of our interactions, 174
    power dynamic and, 178
    understanding where child is
        coming from and, 176–77
nicotine use, 226–28
nonverbal communication/messages,
        134, 193

nonverbal role-modeling, 151–52
nutrition, 99, 218

O
online activity, socialization and,
 219–20. *See also* social media
oppositional defiant disorder, 213
overreaction, controlling oneself
 from, 38–39

P
parent(s). *See also* evolving families
 arguing in front of their children,
 150
 being friend of their child, 189
 as change agents, 26–29
 child's needs from, xviii–xix
 counteracting societal influences,
 xvi
 emotional and mental control of,
 75
 fighting in front of the children,
 150
 hybrid model of parenting and, 39
 influence on child's sense of self,
 25
 listening to intuition of, 225–26,
 227–28
 mastering skills they would like
 to role-model, 149–51
 power of. *See* power and power
 dynamics
 proactivity in, 127
 progressiveness in, 127–28

role in child's issues, 12–13
role-modeling by. *See* role-
 modeling/models
sense of stability provided by,
 xii–xiii
substance abuse by, 7–8
supervision by, 82–83
supporting each other, 64
SWEEP done by, 93–106
upbringing of. *See* childhood
 experiences (parent)
parenting
answering questions about your, 43
beginning with you, 17, 22–25
child(ren) influencing how you
 see your, 43–44
commitment and motivation for
 successful, 21–22
comparing and contrasting your
 parents' parenting with your
 own, 47–48
in evolving families, 191–97
giving yourself credit for positive
 steps in, 208–9
helping child become self-
 directed, 157–58
hybrid model of, 39–40, 43
questioning foundation of your, 40
questions to answer about your
 parents', 44–47
by stepparents, 199–200
understanding influences from
 your family history and,
 14–17

parenting dashboard, 76–85

parenting goals, parents realigning
their, 23–24, 28–29

parenting partner. *See also* evolving
families

child's view of, in evolving
families, 189–90

fighting with, in front of
children, 11, 150

partnership with, in evolving
families, 191–93

regaining parenting power and
working with, 65–66

parenting style(s)

adjusting, on parenting
dashboard, 76–77

Balanced Parent, 85–87

Feather Parent, 80–84

importance of understanding
each, 76

Seesaw Parent, 84–85

Tyrant Parent, 77–80

parents (of adults)

blaming your, 37

changing the lens of how you
view, 43–47

comparing and contrasting your
parenting with parenting by
your, 47–48

duplicating or avoiding approach
of, 40

questions about parenting by,
44–47

passive-aggressiveness, 15

pediatricians, 218

perfection, expecting, 160

permanence, 30

accepting child's individuality
and, 120

child's need for, 10–11

in evolving families, 189, 191

Feather Parent and, 80

parental self-control and, 75

parents regaining power and, 65

phone. *See* smartphones

physical safety, 10, 11, 30

play and leisure time, 103–4

police, xi, 52, 73, 213, 215

positive self-talk, 138

power and power dynamics

communicating with children
about changes in, 63–65

consistency in practicing
boundaries and, 67

erosion of parental, 53–57

Family Power Questionnaire,
61–62

influence of child's power and,
55–56

money and, 59–60

negotiation and, 177, 178

parents regaining their, 57–58,
60–61, 62–69

reasons for shift in, 57

Tyrant Parent and, 79

underlying causes of power
struggles, 63

praising your child, 117–18

privacy issues, 210–11
proactivity, 127
progressiveness, 127–28, 179
psychiatrists, 216–17, 218
psychoeducational testing, 161, 226, 227
psychotherapy, individual, 63
punishment(s), 207–8

Q
quality time with your child, 118, 194–95
questions
    about what defines and enriches your family, xvii
    about your childhood and your parenting, 40
    about your parenting, 43–44
    about your parents' actions, 44–48
    about your reaction to your child's misbehavior, 41
    asked about your ex, 197–98
    asked of medical professionals, 217, 218
    asked to child, 142, 162–63
    to clarify sender's message, 135
    to family members about your family, 123–24
    family power questionnaire, 61–62
    in self-inventory, 30–32

R
random drug testing, 215–16
rebound relationships, 195–97

red flags, xv, 9, 37, 48, 105, 206–7, 214, 219, 225, 228
rehab, 7, 86, 230
reset button, hitting the, xiv, xvi, xviii, 228
resilience, building, 164–65
respect
    Balanced Parent and, 86
    in blended families, 199
    communication and, 136
    curfews and, 68
    Feather Parent and, 81
    parental self-control and, 75–76
    role-modeling, 150
    for your child, 218–19
rewards, 159–60
Ritalin, 227
rituals
    cultural, 124, 125
    dinnertime, 142–43
role-modeling/models, 9, 25, 147–54
    acknowledging missteps in behavior and, 154
    actions speaking louder than words and, 151–53
    of behavior versus words, 153–54
    behavior you would like to see, 148–51
    in communication, 101, 136
    eating habits, 99
    getting enough sleep and, 96
    grabbing opportunities for, 152–53
    humor and, 140–41

role-modeling/models (*cont.*)

impact of, 147–48

the kind of person you would want your child to become, 223

love of learning, 161

lying and, 206

negotiations, 175

responsible relationship with alcohol, 212

SWEEP and, 104, 107, 223

vulnerability and, 142

"Roses and Thorns" game, 142

routines, 118, 194

rules. *See also* law, breaking the

in family portrait, 115

following through on, 82

for screen time, 82

Tyrant Parent and, 77, 80

S

sadness, 218

safety

accepting child's individuality and, 120

brain development and threat to, 74–75

child(ren)'s need for, 10–11

curfews and, 68

disciplining your child who is bigger than you, 215

emotional, in evolving families, 191

in evolving families, 189, 191

Feather Parent and, 80, 81

Identified Patient responding to lack of, 12

parental supervision and, 82–83

parents regaining power and, 65

power dynamic erosion and, 57

Seesaw Parent and, 85

sense of stability and, xii–xiii

social media activity and, 211

school(s) and academics

acknowledging successes in, 159

addressing issues that involve, 108

being late for picking up from, 42–43

contacting Los Angeles County Department of Children and Family Services Child Protection, 5–6

Covid-19 pandemic and, 97, 220–21

focus on process of learning versus rewards in, 159–60

parent projecting issues onto son about, 73–74

parents meeting with administrators of, 63

questions about your child's environment in, 97

red flag of improvement in, 225, 226

responding to your child's difficulties in, 160–61

screen time, rules for, 82

secrecy, 9, 198, 206

security
    evolving families and, 195
    Feather Parent and, 83, 84
    quality time with children and
        their feeling of, 118
Seesaw Parent, 84–85
self-confidence
    allowing child to be in the
        "driver's seat" and, 158
    child's self-expression and, 143
    hobbies and, 104
self-control, 136
self-esteem
    basic needs for developing
        healthy, xviii–xix
    being present for your child and,
        117
    dissolution of marriage and,
        195–96
    parent's interactions with their
        child influencing their, 25
    parent's role-modeling and, 147
    providing positive encouragement
        for, 161–63
self-inventory
    parents on the same page after
        doing a, 28–29
    parents realizing their need to do
        a, 26–28
    questions for, 29–32
    reason for doing a, 32–33
    unpacking your baggage and,
        38–40
self-medicating, 213–14

sexual identity, acceptance of your
    child's, 120
sibling (parent's), exercise on your
    childhood done with, 44–47
sleep, 5, 63, 95–96, 107–8, 226
smartphones, 176–77, 210–11
socialization, online activity and,
    219–20
social media
    children not allowing you to
        follow them on, 211–12
    increased use during Covid-19
        pandemic, 102–3
    looking at your child's accounts,
        210–11
social/separation anxiety, 219–20
Sophy Method, 94, 133. *See also*
    SWEEP
stability, sense of, xii–xiii
    child(ren) not raised with, 9
    evolving families and, 189, 190
    parental self-control and, 75
stepparents, 199–201
stimulants, 227–28
stories, family, 124
strengths
    acknowledging your child's,
        117–18
    consistency in encouraging your
        child's, 163–64
    discovering and cultivating a
        child's, 157–58, 163
    identifying child's, 33
    supporting your child's, 122–23

structure, child's need for, xix

substance use/abuse

    finding drugs in child's bag, 213–14

    letting your child drink at home and, 212–13

    marijuana use, 5–7, 11

    by parents, 7–8

    power dynamic imbalance and, 58–59

    rehab, 7, 86, 230

suicide/suicidality, xv, 99, 216–17, 230

SWEEP, 209, 214, 226, 231

    Covid-19 and, 215

    creating a road map after doing a, 107–9

    eating, 98–100

    emotional expression, 100–103

    finding drugs in your child's bag and, 214

    identifying areas for betterment and, 107–9

    medical support and, 105–6

    motivation for learning and, 220–21

    play, 103–4

    role-modeling and, 104, 107, 223

    sleep, 95–96

    teaching your child to do a, 104–5

    work, 96–98

T

talents, supporting a child's, 121

tantrums, 65, 217–18

target behavior(s), 179, 182, 183

therapy

    couples, 59

    family, 58, 63

    individual psychotherapy, 63

time-outs, 207–8

trauma, brain development and, 15, 74–75

trust

    Balanced Parent and, 86

    communication and, 136

    curfews and, 68

    random drug testing and, 215–16

    Seesaw Parent and, 85

Tyrant Parent, 77–80

U

unchaperoned parties, 86

unpacking and repacking baggage

    hybrid parenting and, 38–40

    lessons learned from, 41–43

    parenting style and, 74

    questions to help with, 44–47

    reactions to your child's poor behavior and, 40–41

V

values. *See also* family portrait

    aligning parenting with your, xviii, xxi

in family portrait, 113

importance of building and living out your family's, 231–32

questioning your, 32

reframing, as evolving family, 191

role-modeling and, 148, 153

talking about your family's, 123

vaping, 226–27

vulnerability, 164–65

W

well-being

assessment tool for evaluating, 63, 93. *See also* SWEEP

of child in evolved families, 192

whiteboard, 64, 172, 231

work

child's experience in school, 97

Covid-19 pandemic's impact on, 96–97

explained, 96

finding time for your child and, 116–17

improving your situation with, 108

Y

yelling

changing your child's behavior of, 148

shift in power dynamics and, 66

yes/no responses, 210